Secrets from the Casting Couch

On Camera Strategies for Actors from a Casting Director

Nancy Bishop
Illustrations by Bonnie Glover

methuen | drama

Methuen Drama

3   5   7   9   10   8   6   4   2

First published in Great Britain in 2009 by Methuen Drama

Methuen Drama
A & C Black Publishers Ltd
36 Soho Square
London W1D 3QY
www.methuendrama.com

A CIP catalogue record for this book is available from the British Library

ISBN 978 1 408 11327 1

Cartoon illustrations © Bonnie Glover

Typeset by RefineCatch Limited, Bungay, Suffolk
Printed and bound in Great Britain by Martins the Printers

Table of contents

Contents

Acknowledgements

Thanks to: Derek Power, Joel Kirby, Paul Engelhardt, David Rowland, Meg Liberman, Maureen Duff, John and Ros Hubbard, Suzanne Smith, Lucinda Syson, Tammy Rosen, Jeremy Conway, Fred Roos, Frank Moiselle, Priscilla John, Andy Pryor, Beatrice Kruger, Karin Dix, Lina Todd, Sheila Jaffe, Dramatics Magazine, Louise Bolton, Emma Style, Minna Pyykala, Olga Zahorbenska, Zuzka Milkova, Jack Davidson, Sarka Hudeckova, Emil Linka at Storm Bohemia, Bonnie Gillespie, David Minkowski, Matthew Stillman, Bernard Hiller, Chris Rourke and User Vision, at the Casting Scene, Spotlight, Deborah DeWitt, Jimmy Watson and Mark Coleman at the Actors Bothy, Raw Talent Productions, Adelle Robins, Chuck Harper. All of the actors who have auditioned with me and taken my workshops. Kenny, Leni, and Dad.

Permissions

Alien Vs Predator, written by Dan O'Bannon, Ronald Shusett, directed by Paul Anderson, Twentieth Century Fox.

Anne Frank: The Whole Story, written by Kirk Ellis, directed by Robert Dornhelm, ABC Productions.

Before Sunset, written by Richard Linklater, Kim Krizan, Julie Delpy, Ethan Hawke, directed by Richard Linklater, Warner Independent Pictures.

Blade II, written by David Goyer, directed by Guillermo del Toro, Revolution Studios.

The Bourne Identity, written by Tony Gilroy, W. Blake Herron, directed by Doug Liman, Universal Pictures.

Euro Trip, written by Alec Berg, David Mandel, Jeff Schaffer, directed by Jeff Schaffer, DreamWorks.

Hitler: The Rise of Evil, written by John Pielmeier, directed by Christian Duguay, CBS Productions.

Tristan and Isolde, written by Dean Georgaris, directed by Kevin Reynolds, Scott Free Productions.

Every effort has been made to trace and acknowledge copyright owners. If any right has been omitted the publishers offer their apologies and will rectify this in subsequent editions following notification.

Preface

I met Nancy Bishop while we were working together on *Last Holiday* for Paramount Pictures. While I was casting between New York, Los Angeles and New Orleans, Nancy was hustling up actors between France, Germany, England and the Czech Republic. Nancy understands the casting process on both sides of the Atlantic. She knows and has worked with some of the best actors, directors, and casting directors from all over the world. In *Secrets from the Casting Couch*, she uses this international perspective to offer actors concrete advice about how to approach auditioning in front of camera.

Secrets from the Casting Couch is the most comprehensive book I've seen for actors confronting the casting process. Auditioning is a specific skill. Actors have limited time to prepare a believable performance that will result in a job. Nancy understands the demands that auditioning makes on actors and with a sense of humor and a direct style, she offers positive strategies for success.

We casting directors, during our work process, are not always at liberty, nor do we have the time to answer the many queries that actors might have. The reality is that casting is a stressful process for the casting director as well as for the actors. I appreciate that Nancy has taken the time to write this book that answers a wide range of questions that actors often ask. Her prose, peppered with amusing stories from the trenches, provides essential information that every actor should know.

Secrets from the Casting Couch emphasizes a central truth in casting; casting directors are intrigued with an actor's essence, not just their acting ability. Actors often regard the audition as a 'test', but in truth the most important thing is for them to bring themselves to the scene. When an actor is himself, we see how his chemistry combines with the character. An example of this is when I was casting *The Sopranos* for HBO. I knew as I was reading the script that James Gandolfini (not famous at the time) was the one who would play the role. Tony Soprano is a character that the audience loves to hate. So even though Tony is a bad guy, the audience has to like him. He has to have a sense of humor and a humanity with which the audience can connect. James won the role because he brought his vulnerabilities and his sense of humor; in short he brought his own self to the audition process. It was his true personality, his essence if you will, that ultimately fitted with the written character and created the Tony Soprano that we all know and love.

Actors should also take an interest in Part 3, in which Nancy clearly sets out the professional ways for actors to market themselves. A talented actor can miss the boat if he doesn't present himself well; we easily pass over poor headshots and muddled resumes. She also rightly points out the prevalence of the internet in the casting process, and the possibilities that it offers for actors to make their work known.

In short, I am happy to recommend *Secrets from the Casting Couch*, because when actors are well prepared, it ultimately makes my job as a casting director easier as well.

Sheila Jaffe, Casting Director
2009

Introduction

Acting is not just an art, it's a craft

This book has come to life because I know so many actors who say, 'I'm just bad at auditioning'. There are many excellent actors who perform poorly at castings. Why? Because they haven't learned the skills. You may also be bad at hunting, but if you live in the jungle, you'll starve. It doesn't matter how great an actor you are. If you don't know how to get the jobs, you won't have an acting career.

Secrets from the Casting Couch is designed for three types of actors: actors just starting out who wish to learn success strategies for the casting process; experienced actors making the transition from theatre into film; and experienced actors who frequently audition but aren't landing the role.

There are many successful theatre actors who don't make it in film castings because they don't know the on-camera techniques. When we were shooting *Euro Trip* in Prague, I read a famous Czech theatre actor. When the directors met him, they loved his performance. I thought it was a done deal, and was shocked when he didn't even make the short list. When I asked why, the directors said that he was flat on screen. It didn't matter that they loved him in person.

It's a myth that some actors have 'it' in front of camera and other actors don't. While it's true that some people are naturally more 'watchable' on screen, there are skills that actors can learn to develop and improve screen presence. When you first learned to drive a car, you didn't just head into rush hour traffic. You had to learn and practise. Screen acting, and auditioning requires the same type of training and commitment.

Secrets also addresses the internet and home video age. I've worked on films where many of the actors were cast on the strength of a self-audition, where an actor films his read and sends it to a casting director, via the internet or post. The most famous example of a successful self-audition is Elijah Wood in *Lord of the Rings*. Video cameras aren't expensive, so if you're serious about working in film or TV, you should own a camera, and know how to use it on yourself. As painful as the process may be, the only way to improve your screen acting skills is by watching and evaluating yourself *on camera*.

The good news is that casting is not just about luck. Nature didn't dole out good casting genes in the DNA of certain actors and not in others. Auditioning, like acting itself, is not just an art — it is a craft. A craft can be learned, practiced and perfected. There is no mystery to it. *Secrets* teaches practical techniques for improving your audition method.

I come from a theatre background and fell into casting by accident. I learned about film acting by directing castings for supporting talent on nearly sixty major studio and network projects to date. Through the years I have broken down casting into a system of techniques and strategies that I teach at casting workshops throughout Europe and the US. In these pages you will learn this system.

Good auditioning can't be learned solely from a book: you have to practise, practise, and practise more. Ballet dancers start their warm up doing bar work. Then they dance for hours, every day. They return again and again to ballet class. Piano players start with scales, followed by hours and hours of practice, alone in a room until their hands ache. Yet there are wannabe actors whose idea of warming up before a casting is to drink coffee and read a newspaper.

According to Daniel Levitin, author of *This is Your Brain*, to become a master; a musician needs to practise 10,000 hours. He uses the example of Wolfgang Amadeus Mozart, the child prodigy. Mozart's father was an ambitious composer who pushed his son from a young age. If Mozart started playing for 32 hours a week from the age of two, then he'd have done 10,000 hours by the age of eight — so much for the myth of the genius with the God given gifts. He had to work for it. It is vitally important for the actor, just like the dancer, the musician, or any artist, to continually hone their skills. That means practising alone for hours, but it also means getting outside guidance, coaching, and commitment to learning new acting techniques etc. What are the scales or the bar work for the actor? What is the equivalent? There are exercises that actors can do daily to sharpen their technique and I have suggested some in Part 4.

I will not pretend to offer a formula for success because there is none. I can offer strategies, but for each 'rule' there will be an exception. For example, I would generally say that an actor should prepare well for a casting. But it's a crazy business. There will be times when an actor will prepare like mad, then another actor who, without having read the text, will book the role instead. Showbiz ain't fair.

The 'secret' in the book's title is that there is no secret. To excel you need to work hard and never stop studying the craft. Auditioning means going to battle in an ultra-competitive arena. It's not for the feint of heart. It is, in fact, for the terminally insane. But if you've decided that you're crazy enough to join the carnival, then welcome to this book.

Part 1

Success strategies for casting

The top eleven list

Actors who get cast are actors who . . .

1. Enjoy casting
2. Prepare
3. Make choices
4. Act and react in the moment
5. Play in the eyes
6. Possess an inner monologue
7. Commit to the scene
8. Stake a claim on the role, take a risk
9. Tell the story
10. Listen
11. Wag their tails

Over my years of casting work, I've contemplated why certain actors succeed at castings, while others, maybe equally talented actors, have not. What did the winning actors do in the casting process that 'worked?' In the following chapters in Part 1, I've listed the top eleven strategies.

1 Enjoy casting

> *Nothing great has ever been achieved without enthusiasm.*
>
> Ralph Waldo Emerson, Philosopher

Actors who get cast are actors who enjoy the casting process. When I was casting *Dune* for the Science Fiction Channel, I met one talented actress, Anna Rust, for the role of Alia. We called her back to read with us a few times. In the end we decided that she was a little too young for the role (she was only four at the time). When I told her father that unfortunately we had not chosen Anna, he said, 'It doesn't matter. She thinks she already did the film'.

In a sense Anna was right. She did have the role. For those few minutes when she came in for her initial meetings, she was playing Alia in front of camera, for an audience of three; myself, my assistant, and the camera operator. We then showed it to the producer and the director. The casting was a film in itself. She played Alia in a mini-film. Anna did eventually book roles in *The Brothers Grimm* and *Doctor Zhivago*. Her story drives home the importance of attitude. There are plenty of things that an actor doesn't have control over in the casting process but one thing that they always have control of is their attitude. Having a persistent, positive and professional approach is at least fifty percent of the game. Anna succeeded for two reasons, both related to attitude. First because she enjoyed the process, and second because she approached the casting as if she already had the role.

The old adage in theatre is that if the performer is enjoying himself, so will the audience. The same goes in a film casting. Enjoy it and we will too. If casting

Some actors see casting directors as executioners

is an excruciating experience for an actor, you can guarantee that it's a painful experience for the casting director as well. No one wants to work with an actor who is miserable and down on themselves, yet some actors approach casting as an execution. If you come to the audition, as if to your death, then we may put you out of your misery — 'Thank you. Next!' On the other hand, if you're enjoying the process, then we may ask for more.

Casting is an intrinsic part of the actor's life. There are a few super stars in the world who don't have to test, but even top actors still have to read for roles. Johnny Depp had to prove to studio executives that he could sing before playing in *Sweeney Todd*. Daniel Craig had to read for *Bond*. Marlon Brando famously had to screen test for *The Godfather*.

If you dislike casting, then you're going to dislike being an actor. Find a way to make friends with this process. Talented actors get turned down at castings all the time. Why? Because there's only one role and many actors. But each time an actor comes to read, she is building a relationship with directors that can eventually lead to a role. Here's a lesson from Thomas Watson, founder of IBM, one of the most successful men in the world: 'If you want to increase your success rate, double your failure rate'. To succeed, you have to fail even more. Jack Nicholson had to audition five times to get into Lee Strasberg's acting studio in New York, and Harvey Keitel a whopping eleven times.

Certainly it's not easy putting yourself on the line again and again. An actor going to castings day after day without any success can easily begin to doubt her skills. Thoughts such as: 'I never get roles'; 'This director doesn't like me'; 'I messed up my last audition'; 'I've already been to six castings this week and no one wants me' can begin to take over. These attitudes are killers that infect performance and poison effectiveness.

Instead, think about the things you're good at. If you're a good cook, the chances are that you like cooking. If you're an excellent skier, you probably love skiing. It works the other way too. If you love skiing, then you're a good skier. If you like casting, you're good at it. If you're good at it, you enjoy it. Remember casting commandment number one: Enjoy thy casting.

Transform your nerves into enthusiasm

> *The entertainer's journey through fear is the burden and the blessing of performance: it's what invests the enterprise with bravery, even a kind of nobility.*[1]
>
> Jonathan Lair

When you are nervous, it means that you care and that you're invested in the outcome. Nerves are not only a positive sign, they are a condition of success. It's the dizzying sense of fear that can either launch your audition to the

---

[1] *The New Yorker,* 28 Aug 2006. 'The nightmare of stage fright.'

next level or reduce you to distress. If you're nervous, then make nerves your ally. Nervousness is energy. Transform your anxiety into enthusiasm. To be enthusiastic originally meant to be possessed by a god or inspired by a celestial source. Enthusiasm is that inner energy that fuels our love for our art. Bring it with you and create a divine performance.

Enthusiasm does not mean you have to kiss up to the auditors or fetch the director's slippers. Rick Pagano, who has cast episodes of *24*, instructs actors to enter the casting with a professional distance, for which they will be respected. An over-willingness to please and be liked by your auditors can generate negative nerves that will overwhelm your performance. Successful actors are not desperate for the job. You're not there to prove anything. We already know you're an actor. That's why you've been invited to the casting. Read for the role the way a star does — as if you already have the role. Claim the casting and the space and time it takes to do your work, then gracefully exit.

Bring your personality with you

> *Most actors come into the interview situation wearing a thick mask, spending their energies to protect themselves. It's rough interviewing someone who is determined to keep himself hidden.*
>
> Michael Shurtleff, Broadway Casting Director[2]

Sometimes actors leave their personality behind when they come in the door. I've witnessed many actors who normally possess a well-developed sense of humor, entering with a stone face. Why? Personality is so important to our profession. Remember that it's a job interview as well as a reading. No one wants to work with an actor who has no sense of humor or personality. You don't have to concentrate on being charming, just on being yourself. 'You're doing an autobiography every time,'[3] said Dustin Hoffman. How can you do an autobiography if you've forgotten yourself?

[2] Shurtleff, Michael. *Audition: Everything an Actor Needs to Know to Get the Part.* Walker and Company, New York, 1978.
[3] Inside the Actors Studio, James Lipton, Bravo TV.

Personality is what gets an actor the role. I don't mean that people with fun-loving personalities get cast and those who are grumpy don't. Often directors are looking for a quality, an essence, a part of that actor's chemistry that fits with the role. They may be seeking, for example, a lightness, a heaviness, a world-weariness, a bounciness, that *je ne sais quoi* which makes us individuals. The great acting teacher Michael Chekhov called it 'individual atmosphere'. There's an alchemy to casting that's beyond the thespian's reach. While actors like to think that they are perfect for every role, director Stephen Frears, speaking at a talent campus event at the Berlin Film Festival in 2009, described the director's 'opposite philosophical position'. We're interested in what your quality is — there's nothing you can do about it.

At a certain point in the casting process, there will be at least a handful of actors who can play any given role. From that short list, the performer who gets cast is the one who projects the quality that fits with the director's vision of the character. John Wayne spoke of film acting as 'pushing your personality through'. Film director Bernardo Bertolucci says that each face has a secret, a mystery, and through his work he seeks to unlock the mystery in the faces he casts.

Acting coach Bernard Hiller uses the analogy of an ice cream cone. According to Hiller, every actor brings her own unique flavor to the role. That's what interests casting directors. What flavor are you bringing? You are bringing yourself. Even imperfections can get an actor the role. Actor Pete Postlethwaite has made a living from a scarred, pockmarked face. Sometimes it is the thing we are the most insecure about, our imperfections, that distinguish us from the rest.

Bare yourself

The act of performance always involves vulnerability. Look to the ancient roots of theatre. In ancient Greece, theatre was a religious rite, a ritual. The performance was a sacrificial act in which the actors went forth in front of the community to experience the pain and pathos of tragedy. Thespians acted out the horrors — the deaths, the bloody fratricides, the betrayals — in place of ordinary citizens, to purge the audience of these atrocities. Performance is terrifying because it involves baring oneself. A psychological survey revealed that speaking in public is what people fear the most, even more than death. Yet performers do this every day. Performing takes great courage because it demands the actor's vulnerability. Be courageous enough to expose yourself in the casting process, warts and all.

> *According to most studies, people's number one fear is public speaking. Number two is death. Death is number two. Does that sound right? This means to the average person, if you go to a funeral, you're better off in the casket than doing the eulogy.*
>
> Jerry Seinfeld

Things to remember from this chapter

* Enjoy the casting

* Transform your nerves into enthusiasm

* Make friends with the process

* Approach the casting as if you've already playing the role

* Bring your personality with you

* Allow yourself to be vulnerable

2 Prepare

An Actor Prepares was the title of Konstantin Stanislavski's first book. Opinions vary about this early twentieth century Russian director who is credited with revolutionizing acting and founding what we now call 'method acting'. Some acting teachers now find his method dated or believe that he has been misinterpreted. Many actors have moved on to new training programs such as Anne Bogart's Viewpoints and Sanford Meisner's technique (an offshoot of Stanislavski). Regardless of how we feel about Stanislavski, his basic approach to a role fits screen auditioning perfectly. When you are given a side (a section of the script) for an audition, what is the first thing you do? Do you just highlight and memorize your lines? You need to scan the text for information that will help you play the role, concentrating on key facts that will fuel your choices in a short amount of time. Stanislavski stresses establishing the facts of the scene by asking the 'W' questions:

* Who am I?
* Where am I?
* Who am I talking to?
* What do I want?
* Where are the changes? (OK, I added this one.)

> *In transmitting the facts and plot of a play the action involuntarily transmits its inner content.*
>
> Konstantin Stanislavski[1]

[1] Stanislavski, Konstantin. Translated by Elizabeth Reynolds Hapgood. *Creating a Role*. Routledge, 1948.

No one can act in a vacuum. It is amazing to me how many actors come into a casting without having done this very basic homework. This is Acting 101, and when I teach this in my audition technique classes, the actors roll their eyes, thinking how dare I bore them with such basics. But every time the actors who don't perform well — and they can be experienced professionals — are the ones who have neglected these basic choices.

How do you get the answers if you can't read the entire script? The first thing you should do is ask for a copy. It's true that in film castings it is not always possible to read the entire script; Woody Allen doesn't even give out the title of his films during the casting process. If this is the case, you may be surprised how much you can learn by reading just one scene in a script. Most of the information you need will be embedded in the scene. Hopefully your agent will also provide a brief synopsis of the plot, prepared by the casting director. See Part 5 for examples of scene analysis. Certainly the scene will provide at least basic answers to these questions. Work with what you know; that's all you need and that's all any of the actors have, so you're all in the same position.

If you really feel like you can't answer these questions, you can ask the casting director when you're in the casting. I respect actors who ask questions. It reflects a thoughtful and professional approach.

Who am I?

Who's there?

First line of *Hamlet* by William Shakespeare

Identity. This is the first question in drama. The answer could be simple. I am an American teenager traveling through Europe. I am a madame of a bordello. I am a scientist. While it's important to answer the question, it's equally important not to over-analyze. This is an instance when Stanislavski's method, or its misinterpretation, is over-wrought at an audition. I've seen actors prepare a long list of questions about a character; what is the character's favorite color, what does she eat for breakfast etc. For a casting call, stick to the basics. Time is limited. Don't go into too much detail about the character or you obfuscate your objectives.

Here's a scene I cast from *Blade II*, written by David Goyer and directed by Guillermo del Toro, produced by Revolution Studios.

Scene 1
Int. community blood bank — entrance — night

JARED NOMAK, *20s feverish and strung-out, in serious need of a fix.He carries a small plastic bag overflowing with what must be all of his possessions.*

NURSE [OS]: Jared Nomak?
> *Nomak looks up. We get a better look at his face now — he has a thin vertical scar running from his lower lip to his chin. A* NURSE *smiles and motions for him to join her. She's carrying a clipboard.*

NURSE: We're ready for you now.
> *Nomak follows the* NURSE *into a dimly lit hallway. We track their progress in a convex safety mirror suspended from the hallway ceiling.*

NURSE: Where did you get that scar on your chin?

NOMAK: Childhood accident.

NURSE: [*referring to her clipboard*] You say you don't have any immediate next of kin? Is that right?

NOMAK: Not that I'm in contact with.
> *He observes a* WHITE-TILED CHAMBER *where blood is being hosed off the floor by men in white coveralls and plastic boots.*

NURSE: Nobody to call in case of an emergency?

NOMAK: No. Does that mean I can't be a donor?

NURSE: It depends. We came up with some unusual results on your blood test.

NOMAK: How unusual?

> NURSE: Your blood has a very rare phenotype. One we
>   haven't encountered before.
> NOMAK: What are you talking about?
> *The* NURSE *smiles, baring fangs. We realize now that she is a*
> *vampire.*

Here is an example of a character which is quite simple. This nurse is a vampire. The actor doesn't need to do a Freudian analysis of this character's relationship with her mother. She wants to suck Nomak's blood. These main facts are enough to ground the performance in this scene.

Research

Find out as much as possible about the project. Information is power. Is it a historical drama? If the project documents a real period, then this character might have actually lived. There's so much information you can get on the internet, there's no excuse not to do your research. When we were casting *Charles II* for the BBC, almost every character was someone who had lived. Even when you're just reading for a crowd member shouting 'Death to Catholics!' know the context for that period of history. In *Hitler: The Rise of Evil* for CBS, there were actors who came in to read the role of Rudolf Hess without knowing who this historic figure was. They had a harder time acting the role. James Babson, who did the research on Hitler's deputy, got the part.

Where am I?

See the location and play it. Certainly the side will provide the location — are you inside (INT.) or outside (EXT.)? Are you in a public or a private space? The way we relate to our spouses at the kitchen table is different to how we would relate to them in a crowded train station. If there are other people around, maybe you don't want them to hear your conversation. When an actor hasn't answered this question, it shows. They look like they are floating in space.

'Playing the space' is an important concept. For example, I had to audition actors for a scene in *Hellboy* that took place in an underground tunnel. The actors had to imagine that it was dark and wet, and they had to really see the monsters that were coming to swallow them. The actors who were cast were the ones who could see the space and make it real. In the world of CGI (computer generated images), you will frequently experience this on set too. You won't be provided with the dark tunnel and with the monster — all you'll have is a blue screen to play off. Samuel Jackson said of his work on *Star Wars*, 'They put you in a big blue room and say "fight 'em". So you put your little kid hat on and fight 'em.'[2]

Anchor yourself in the location of the scene. Otherwise your performance will float away

Who am I talking to?

What is your relationship to the other character? Is it your mother? Your lover? Your enemy? Do you like this person? Do you know this person? Your character needs or wants something from the other. This need drives the scene. For example, 'I want this person to love me'.

[2] Inside the Actors Studio, James Lipton, Bravo TV.

Here is a monologue from ABC's *Anne Frank: The Whole Story*, written by Kirk Ellis and directed by Robert Dornhelm. Edith Frank is hiding from the Nazis, cooped up in an attic with her family and another family during World War II.

---

244. Int. annex — Otto/Edith's room

EDITH *and* MIEP *sit on the edge of Edith's bed* . . .

> EDITH: [*after a beat*] You hear how they all talk. 'After the war.' I say nothing. What can I say to them? Mrs. Van Pels — you know how she carries on. Who is she to criticize? The things she says about the children. The children, Miep. Anne. Margot. Otto says we must be hopeful. Hopeful for what?
>
> MIEP: You mustn't think such things, Mrs. Frank.
>
> EDITH: I know. I have to be strong. But for how much longer? If only this waiting would end. At least then I could be certain. Miep — we're not going to make it. No — it will have a bad end, I'm sure of it now. It doesn't matter for me. But the children, Miep. What's to become of the children?

Who is Edith talking to? She's talking to Miep, someone who lives outside the cloistered attic. When I ask my students to figure out what she wants from Miep, they usually make the choice that Edith needs Miep to be her mother now. She needs Miep to do what she's doing all day with her daughters. Edith needs Miep to say, 'You will survive. You're going to make it'. In other words, she desperately needs and wants Miep to disagree with her when she says they're not going to make it.

What do I want?

This is the most important question. The character wants something and that's why we're interested. One of the first great tragedies ever written was about Oedipus who stands at a crossroads. He is in a hurry and there is an obstacle. He makes a decision. He kills a man who stands in his way. The man is his father. He acts out of passion. He wants something. He wants a clear path. The play picks up when there is a plague in Thebes. To lift the plague, a riddle must be solved. Oedipus desperately wants to solve the mystery and lift the plague. The chorus warns him repeatedly not to explore this riddle because it will reveal an unbearable truth — that he has killed his father and married his mother — but Oedipus needs to know all and his need drives the story. Story telling has not changed much from ancient Greek times. Your character, like Oedipus, must want something. There is no acting without objective. Obvious as this might sound, actors often come to auditions without thinking about what the character wants.

Devise an active verb to spring your character into action. To act means to perform an action; that is why actors are so called. This is where many actors fail in a casting. They have gone to acting school and learned about objectives, yet they don't make vital and crucial choices. The best verbs are those that take a direct object. For example, think of the name of the other character. John. I want to kill John, I want to change John, I want to hug John, or I want John to hug me. If you choose a verb that takes an indirect object, it weakens the scene. For example, I want to complain to John. I want to find something out from John. Do you see how those objectives are not as strong, precise and direct? They give you less to play.

Some actors forget to choose an objective because they're so obsessed with their own objective, which is to get the role: they think their objective is to impress the director. This is not your objective! As philosopher Eckhart Toll puts it, 'When you want to arrive at your goal more than you want to be doing what you are doing, you become stressed'. Choose your character's objective and then the scene will work.

Another trick is to look at the page number. It will be on the upper right corner of the script. Be careful not to confuse it with the scene number. Usually a script has about 120 pages so if you're on page 10, you know that you are at the beginning of the film; that tells you that it's an introductory scene. This is the first time we're meeting the character.

Or is it the last scene of a horror movie? That tells us that we've already encountered this monster many times. Looking at the page number gives you an idea of scale and tone. Are we at the end, at the moment of climax, or are the characters being introduced for the first time? Remember that you are a storyteller, so it's important to know where you are in the story.

Where are the changes?

The camera loves change. Change and contrast are built into a good script and exist in almost any scene. Often a change occurs when an actor discovers something. It is always more interesting to see a change on-screen rather than off. I've seen so many actors make their discoveries before they come on, instead of during the scene. Mark where the change happens in the scene. How does it change the scene and the objective? Where does it change? What does the character learn?

Here is a scene from *Tristan and Isolde*[3], a love story like *Romeo and Juliet*. Tristan and Isolde fell in love when she was incognito. They couldn't marry because they were from enemy countries. Now, in an effort for peace, he has fought for her hand in marriage, not for himself but on behalf of his king. Now she must marry his king.

Int. ship's quarters — day

> TRISTAN *enters. He stops at the sight of* ISOLDE *seemingly asleep. He lingers, watching her. When she speaks it shocks him.*

> ISOLDE: Is it because I left? Or is it that you never cared at all?
> *He has no words.*

> ISOLDE: Do you really hate me so much that you'd risk your life to give me to another man—

> TRISTAN: I didn't know it was you!
> *Off her look.*
> You were a lady at Dunluce. Your name was Bragnae . . .
> Your name. I didn't know your name . . .
> *She runs to him, embraces him.*

> ISOLDE: Thank God. Thank God. I thought . . . I thought you didn't love me. I'm sorry, I'm sorry.
> *He continues to allow himself to hold her.*

---

[3] Scott Free Productions, 2006. Written by Dean Georgaris, directed by Kevin Reynolds.

> ISOLDE: You'll stop this then. Say something . . .
> *He pulls back a little.*
> TRISTAN: I can't.
> *It hangs a beat.*
> ISOLDE: What?
> TRISTAN: I must deliver you, otherwise it's war.
> ISOLDE: But I'm yours. You touched me, and I you.
> TRISTAN: It doesn't matter . . .
> ISOLDE: It's the only thing that matters! Tristan, leave with me. I'll go anywhere . . .
> TRISTAN: For God's sakes, don't be naïve! Your marriage will end a hundred years of bloodshed!
> ISOLDE: My marriage to another man.
> TRISTAN: [*sealing his heart*] We will live with this.
> ISOLDE: Don't do this to me! You of all people know I can't bear it . . .
> TRISTAN: We will forget.
> ISOLDE: We won't!

The scene changes twice for Isolde. First, when she learns that he still loves her; this is marked in the script by a hug. The second time is when she discovers that he will not reverse the marriage. The actor decides how to mark the change. You can change objective, strategy, posture, movement, volume, tempo, speed, mood. The audience wants that change. Isolde's first objective can be to *punish* Tristan. Once she learns that he still loves her, her objective is to *fight* for their love.

The audience wants to see Isolde discovering this information. The scene needs to evolve. But caution! Actors who plan their changes, carefully orchestrating each reaction in advance, tend to be mannered. In other words, if the actor playing Isolde sits down before her casting and decides to cry on one line and smile on another and turn their head slightly on another, that's where the performance becomes stale very fast. That's why I have suggested that you make a check mark on the script to mark the change, rather than carefully planning each gesture.

Things to remember from this chapter

Establish the facts of the scene by asking the five 'W' questions.

* Who am I?

* Where am I?

* Who am I talking to?

* What do I want?

* Where does the scene change?

3 Make choices

> When you 'discover a simple, actable goal for yourself . . .
> you are less likely to be confounded or humiliated by an
> ignorant or arrogant director or casting agent.' (sic)
>
> David Mamet, *True and False*

An actor who gets cast is an actor who makes choices. Make an actable choice that is clear to you and easy to play. Keep it simple. Actors tend to make complicated choices that are difficult to play. For example, 'I think I love her, but I'm not sure'. A more decisive and playable choice would be 'I love her and I want to make love to her right now'. This objective is specific and there is a strong image that guides it. Do not choose negative objectives because they are not active and are harder to play. 'I don't want to talk to him,' is a weak choice because it doesn't give you anything to play. In fact, it gives you a reason to leave, but you need a reason to stay in the scene. A more active and therefore easier to play choice is, 'I want to punish to him'.

'I want to leave,' is a particularly weak choice because then you would just leave. It's more interesting to explore what is keeping you from leaving. In Stanislavski's terms that is called the obstacle. Is it because you still love him? If we have a crush on someone but don't tell them, then what is keeping us from telling them? What's at stake? What do we have to lose if we tell them? Rejection? Manhood? Self esteem? Pride?

An actor I know once told me, 'When a man and a woman get married, the husband wants his wife to stay the same and she always changes. The wife, on the other hand, wants her husband to change, and he always stays the same'. Take the wife's perspective when making your choices. Will the other character to change. Prove to him that you're right and he's wrong. Drama involves a competition between two characters.

What are the stakes?

According to an ancient Asian parable, 'A tiger chased a rabbit. The tiger was running for its meal. The rabbit ran for its life. The rabbit lived.' The rabbit had more at stake than the fox. In your audition, be the rabbit, not the fox. Make the choices where the character has the most to lose, the most at stake.

A strong choice is easier to play. At a casting workshop, an actor was performing a blank scene (see Part 5) and he had not bothered to make any choices about why he was on stage, what his motivation was, what he was playing. He had decided who he was and where he was (on a couch with his girlfriend) but had not decided what he wanted. So the performance was flat and lifeless. I asked him to do the scene again but to decide what he wanted. The second time the scene was equally dead. I asked what he had chosen and he said, 'I wanted her to go get ice cream'. Unless he was hypoglycemic and in risk of dying from lack of sugar, this was a very uninspired choice, as well as being inactive and difficult to play. Think about stakes. What is at stake for the character? What has he got to lose? What will happen if she doesn't get the ice cream? In his scenario, not much. In the hypoglycemic scenario, then his life was at stake.

Films are often about sex and violence. Contrary to popular belief, this is nothing new. Sex and violence on screen (or on stage) has existed for all of recorded history, evidenced in ancient Roman theatre, the blood and gore of the Jacobean stage, as well as today's slasher movies. Therefore choices involving sex ('I want to get her into bed') and violence ('I want to kill him') are often appropriate. Even in more subtle genres, the characters' motives can almost always be deduced to these most basic terms — a fight for power, survival, love, or money. Go for the strongest choices possible and they will drive your performance.

David Mamet has good advice in his book *True and False*. 'The "objective" is an action which is fun to do and is something like that which the writer intended.' He is drawing from Stanislavski who said that the objective 'should have attraction for the actor, making him wish to carry it out'. But it has to be something that makes sense in the circumstances of the film. In my class, some actors were working on *The Bourne Identity* scene (see Part 6). I noticed that the scene seemed very strange. They decided that Bourne had just killed Marie's brother. I asked what justification they had to believe that. It turns out that they were trying to follow my instruction to make an interesting choice, where a lot was at stake. OK, interesting yes, but don't make random choices. You need to serve the writer, the story, and the facts of the scene.

The casting differs from work on set because it is an opportunity to make diverse choices. Once you have the role, you are expected to do the scene the same way, more or less, each time. On set, the director will establish a master shot, and then she will shoot it from different angles and in close up. To play it differently each time will disrupt the flow of the scene.

At a casting, however, I would recommend the opposite. Make at least two different choices for the scene before you come in. If you get multiple takes, try it a different way each time. Experiment with the script as you would in a rehearsal. The casting director might suggest trying it again a different way. She might not suggest an idea. This may be because you're the fifty-ninth person in that day, and she's exhausted, or it could be because she wants you to be the brilliant one. You're the artist, so come in with ideas. She might also direct you to play the scene in a certain way and then you have to adapt to her directions, even if they are completely opposite from what you prepared.

Here is an example of a scene from CBS's *Hitler: The Rise of Evil*, written by John Pielmeier. Here Hitler's sister enters the room of her dead daughter, Geli. The sixteen-year-old girl has committed suicide because of Hitler's obsessive control. She speaks to Eva Braun, Hitler's mistress.

Sc. 405D Int. Obersalzburgh House — Geli's Shrine — day

ANGELA *unlocks and opens the door to* GELI's *room.* EVA *steps inside, looks around, frightened a bit, but also fascinated. She reaches for a brush on the dresser, but* ANGELA *warns her:*

> ANGELA: Don't touch. He'll know you've been here.
> *Eva pulls her hand away. Another beat of silence.*

> ANGELA: You can't compete. You're alive and she's a memory.
> His memory. Not mine. Not the real Geli.
> *Fighting tears.*
> I can't bring her back and I can't change what I allowed to
> happen, but I can warn you, Fraulein. If you show any fire,
> any will of your own, he'll turn you into this. This is his
> ideal. Not you. Never you.

If the actor gets three chances to play the scene, what are some different choices she can make?

1. To warn Eva. The subtext would be, 'Get out of this relationship soon or Adolph will kill you, like he did Geli'. This is motivated by concern.

2. To threaten Eva. The subtext: 'Get the hell out of my daughter's room, or I'll kill you'. This is motivated by anger.

3. To scare Eva. Subtext: 'We will all end up like Geli, but there's nothing we can do'. This choice would be motivated by helplessness.

Contrasting choices

Judith Weston in her book *Directing Actors* advises 'Whenever you're not sure what to do with a line, find an opposite. If a scene isn't working, do it wrong'. Although her advice is to directors, it is equally useful to actors. Don't make the obvious choice. Make a contrasting choice. Making a less obvious choice is interesting. Looking for the humor is a good tactic. Find the humor in sad or scary scenes. A sudden nervous giggle in a scene when you're scared out of your wits can be very effective. Conversely, find the pain in a funny scene. Comedy is almost always at someone's expense, and involves deep pain. Your eyes might betray something different than your words The words 'I'm leaving', might mean I love you. The words 'I love you', might mean I'm leaving you. Find the contrasts. Any scene that is about love is also about hate, and vice versa.

As in life, we don't reveal what we mean. In fact, we rarely do. Make sure that you're making the right kinds of choices. Decide what objective to play. Be sure to avoid the pitfall of choosing to play an emotion or a character, over an objective.

An actor who gets cast plays objectives not emotions, adjectives or character. Objectives come first, but be cautious, mistakes can be made.

Mistake no. 1 Playing a character before an objective
Don't judge the character. If you come in thinking, 'This character is nasty, I'm going to play a nasty guy', then you're putting character first. The character doesn't think he's nasty, he's just acting in his own interest. He wants something. Sometimes misguided directors give this type of direction too, 'Play him nastier'. When you hear a direction like that, translate it into actor's language - an action verb; 'I want revenge', for example.

When I was casting *Wanted* for Universal, there was a scene in an early draft of the script (that didn't make it to the final draft) where James McAvoy's character, Wesley, confronts his girlfriend at work. Her boss wants Wesley to get lost. An actor came in to read for the role saying, 'This guy's a jerk'. I reminded him that this wasn't the case; he just didn't want Wesley distracting his worker. But the actor insisted that he was an idiot and proceeded to play him with this judgement. The result was an over the top caricature. I asked him to do it again as himself, without judging the character, and his reading was better, but still with vestiges of the first performance. I didn't have time to work with him further, and sent only the second take to Mindy Marin, the main casting director in LA. She sent notes that he was the right type but he was over-acting. She asked me to call him back and get him to tone it down. For him, character came before objective, and that's why the performance was unbelievable.

In CBS's *Hitler: The Rise of Evil*, Hitler didn't think he was evil, he thought he was saving Germany from impurity. Robert Carlyle had to approach the role not as a bad guy but as a living, breathing person who had goals. He played someone who wanted a pure and glorious Germany. He left it to the audience to judge the character.

Another pitfall is when the script judges the character. One time an actor did a very strange read, and then she asked me whether she should play it more naively. When I looked at the script, I noticed that the screenwriter had decided to describe this character as naive, which was not a helpful note for the actor. I explained that she couldn't play naive and to forget about it. Her performance was much better the second time. 'Naive' is an adjective, not a verb, so it's not an objective.

Mistake no. 2 Putting emotion before objective

> *On the stage there cannot be . . . action which is directed immediately at the arousing of a feeling for its own sake. To ignore this rule results only in the most disgusting artificiality. When you're choosing some bit of action leave feeling and spiritual content alone.*
>
> Konstantin Stanislavski, *An Actor Prepares*

Stanislavski had this advice for stage actors almost one hundred years ago, and actors are still making the same mistakes today. Some actors cry and roll around on the floor, thinking that if they show a lot of emotion it will get them the role. The objective is not to show off your ability to express emotions or tears. If it's appropriate and the tears come, then good. Consider, however, that sometimes in good story telling, we don't need to see the character cry. If you're playing a character whose daughter has just died, you don't have to play sad. The audience knows you're sad. The audience probably just saw the scene when she died. You need to play the character's needs. The sadness may drive the character's goal, but play the goal. When Anthony Hopkins played that wonderfully sad and repressed Mr. Stevens in *The Remains of the Day*, he said, 'I just stood still. I didn't have to cry. I let the audience cry for me'.[1]

There are exceptions to everything, of course. Once I was casting the roles of three college students in *The Prince and Me*. In the scene they had to sit and listen to a corny love story and simply burst into tears. I had to audition actresses who could just cry on cue; that was a time when it was just about playing sad.

---

[1] Inside the Actors Studio, James Lipton, Bravo TV.

Things to remember from this chapter

* Make choices that answer the W questions

* Play high stakes

* Relate your objectives to the author's intention

* Devise at least two different choices for the role

* When possible, make contrasting choices

* Play objectives, not emotions or character

4 Act and react in the moment

> Remember you are part of a team and as in any team,
> you have to collaborate . . . even in a casting session.
> Be careful of that. It's showing patience. If you're in a
> session and the casting director says, 'The director
> is looking for this, let's have a go this way' you need
> to listen.
>
> Lucinda Syson, Casting Director

Be flexible and open to spontaneity. Almost anything can happen at a casting. Don't be thrown by the unexpected. It may be that by the time you get there, the script has already changed and they've cut your role. It's also possible that you mistakenly got the wrong sides or they realize you're better for another part so you get handed another set of sides. You need to be flexible and able to go with it. This is why it's important to exercise your cold reading skills.

This also means being open to a change in your interpretation. You might be playing a psychological lunatic, while the director sees the character as perfectly sane. It's great to make a bold choice, and directors respect that, even if it's the 'wrong' interpretation. You have to be prepared, however, to go in an entirely different direction, and actors fail to do this all the time. An actor will do a nice performance initially, but then they cannot adapt to the director's ideas. Directors are on guard for actors who get stuck in pre-planned line readings. They want the material to sound fresh and un-rehearsed. Some actors over prepare, carefully planning their intonation on each line, driving themselves into a fixed vocal pattern. Prepare enough to be stable, but not so much that you're inflexible.

Sometimes the reader at the casting is as inspiring as a piece of cardboard, reading each line with a dull monotonous voice. This could be intentional because they don't want to influence your performance. In these cases you have to work off of your own energy, or as Michael Caine says, 'If the other actor isn't giving you what you want, act as though they were'.[1] Other times you get a reader who is giving you a performance on the other side because they want to illicit a certain response from you. If you've been rehearsing the scene in a particular way and then the person you are reading with suddenly shouts out one line unexpectedly, do not ignore it. React the way you think the character would react in this situation. As in the theatre, audition performance should be a fluid, flowing, living entity. Part of what the director is testing is your ability to take directions. He might give you a crazy direction just to see if you'll go with it.

The director wants to know that you are listening to him. I once saw a very good actor who was close to getting the role of Ilsa on *Hellboy*, lose the role because she thought it was her job to 'sell' the director her ideas for the role. The director, Guillermo del Toro, had written the script and had a specific vision for how he wanted the role performed. Instead of listening to and incorporating his ideas, she clung to her own interpretation. She was not cast. A director wants an actor who listens. Once you're cast, over and over again, and become a star then you'll get your chance to influence the script, but not in the casting. Come with your own ideas, but be willing to change them to adapt to the whims of the production.

Things to remember from this chapter

* Expect the unexpected

* Stay flexible so you can change your interpretation

* Listen and respond to the director

* Don't expect inspiration from the reader

* Respond to the reader if they are giving you a performance

[1] Caine, Michael. *Acting for Film: An Actor's Take on Movie Making.* Applause Books, New York, 1997.

5 Play in the eyes

> *I have looked into your eyes with my eyes. I have put my heart near your heart.*
>
> Pope John XXIII

Film photographs thought. The thought is in the eyes. If there is one trick in film acting, it is to keep the acting in the eyes. When actors are mugging or overacting in the brow, one effective note is to channel the acting through the eyes, not in the face. When you communicate with your eyes, think with your eyes, listen with your eyes, the camera will love you. Be like Medusa and kill with your eyes. The eye can become as large as eight feet wide on a big screen. When an actor concentrates on communicating with his eyes, then it follows that he will. Getting the brow unfurled is only a slight adjustment and it's about awareness.

LA theatre company, the Actors' Gang, followed by the now defunct New Crimes of Chicago, pioneered a very distinct, Commedia dell'Arte performance style in the 1980s, where the actor would face off directly with the audience, looking straight into an individual spectator's eyes. Their training sessions challenged actors to express strong levels of energy, directing emotions through the eyes and sending them to the audience. The New Crimes Commedia dell'Arte is a highly physicalized form of theatre, accompanied by an insane, thumping rock and roll drumbeat. It seems unlikely that this style could be useful for film acting, which is grounded so fully in realism. Yet the founding members of the Actors' Gang and New Crimes, such as Tim Robbins, John Cusack, and Jeremy Piven have gone on to have fantastically successful film acting careers. I believe that this was in part because they had so much practice with communicating with their eyes.

The form of theatre they practiced is referred to as 'the style'. Original New Crimes member, Adele Robbins, says about her brother, 'Tim believes in the style and always returns to it. It informs everything'. I have adapted some of the training that I got from New Crimes members into an exercise found in Part 5. Although I didn't know it while I was training, 'the style' offered some of the most helpful techniques that I've learned for film acting.

If acting in the eyes is something that doesn't come naturally to you, then join the club. Like anything in acting, it can be practiced and improved. Learn to work with your eyes. Experiment in front of camera. Painters practice by drawing models in the studio, singers sing scales, dancers do pliés, yet there are people who think that without any training at all they can just get in front of camera and act. As the sculptor uses a chisel, so the actor has her eyes. They are your main tool. In a casting be as generous as possible with your eyes, always turning them towards camera. Do not bury your eyes in the script, allowing us to see only your eyelids. Your eyelids are not interesting. Master cold reading techniques that help you look up from the script. Doff the glasses when possible. Wear contacts or do without whenever possible. As the Yiddish proverb goes, the eyes are the mirror of the soul.

Tip

In his seminars to actors, Michael Caine discusses the importance of the eyes in film acting; he suggests that actors get to know their leading eye. Everyone has one eye that is keener than the other. Learn which eye leads and cheat that eye towards the camera. For example if it's your left eye, then focus to the right of camera.

About blinking

In a close up, even a blink registers as a ten on the Richter scale. During my classes when we play back the scenes my actors often say that they're blinking too much. Each actor is bothered by his own blinking on screen, even when the rest of the class doesn't notice. Michael Caine claims that he has trained himself not to blink during close ups. But we all know that our eyes need moisture and that's why we blink, right?

I don't believe it is necessary for an actor to train himself not to blink. Editor Walter Murch has devoted considerable research to the blink. In his book *The Blink of an Eye*, he suggests that the blinking actor provides an opportunity for the editor to cut. He first noticed it when he was editing an early Coppola film, *The Conversation*. 'I kept finding that Gene Hackman would blink very close to the point where I had decided to cut.' So Murch then started to pay acute attention to when and why people blink. 'People will sometimes keep their eyes open for minutes at a time, at other times they will blink repeatedly with many variations in between ... Our rate of blinking is somehow geared more to our emotional state and to the nature and frequency of our thoughts.'[1]

So sometimes when an actor thinks he blinks too much, he is picking up on his own discomfort with the role or performance. If you're focused on the role, the blinks will come at the right time and in the right amount. Trust yourself and stay the course with making choices that help you to identify with the role.

Things to remember from this chapter

* Thought reads in the eyes

* Keep the acting in the eyes and not in the forehead

* Your eyes are your main tool, so learn to use them

* When you focus on the scene, the blinks come at the right times

---

[1] Murch, Walter. *In the Blink of an Eye*. Silman-James Press, Los Angeles, 2001.

6 Possess an inner monologue

When you foster an active and changing, internal monologue, the eyes will be alive.

While less is more is a good adage, doing less can lead to the opposite extreme — dead face. Overacting is the camera's worst nightmare, but dead face is deadly. Dead face is when an actor is not thinking in character and the mind is not engaged; nice house but nobody's home. In other words there is no inner monologue. Ironically this seems to happen most with stage actors who are afraid to overact, so instead they end up doing nothing.

Because many actors fear overacting, casting directors see a lot of safe and frankly dead castings. Overacting is difficult to define but you know it when you see it. Film critics are too lazy to even type it, preferring to use the initials OTT (over the top.) It does not necessarily mean doing 'too much' (whatever that is). If you consider some of the world's favorite actors, Robert de Niro and Jack Nicholson, for example, you will find that they do quite a lot. Examine their performances. The successful actors manage to find stillness while their faces are alive with thought and intention.

Overacting is when an actor mugs (makes faces), and gestures too much. It means that the actor is trying to show the audience what a character is feeling. This performance is not grounded in truth and believability and is poor acting in both film and theatre. The dreaded overacting can also happen when an actor pre-judges a character (also discussed in Chapter 3), or when they get themselves into a pattern of punctuating the lines that becomes fake after a few reads (as discussed in Chapter 4). The antidote to both dead face and overacting is to develop and concentrate on the inner monologue of the character.

The theory goes that for a close up all the actor has to do is think the inner monologue, and the viewer will know; the camera exposes all. Think the character's thought. Michael Caine summarizes it as follows: 'A film actor must think his character's most private thoughts as though no one were watching him'.[1] What works for Michael Caine may not work for you. In my classes, some actors have learned that thinking in character reveals nothing. Even though they insist that they've got an active inner monologue, when they watch the tape they see no light in their eyes, and no wheels turning in their head. (This demonstrates the value of watching oneself on camera occasionally.)

If your face is dead, then you've got to work harder to liven up your inner monologue. French film diva, Jeanne Moreau, claims that, 'Acting is not true to life, it is beyond,' and that actors must 'not only listen but listen beyond'.[2] On camera we don't have to speak louder than in life, but we may have to think louder.

Here is an example from the script *Before Sunset*, written by Richard Linklater, Kim Krizan, Julie Delpy and Ethan Hawke.

8 Ext. garden path stairway — afternoon

They continue to walk/talk

JESSE: No, no, tell me the truth. Did we have problems that night?

CELINE: I was kidding. We didn't even have sex anyway.

JESSE: What? That's a joke, right?

CELINE: No, we didn't. That was the whole thing.

JESSE: Of course we did.

CELINE: But we didn't. You didn't have a condom and I never have sex without one, especially if it was a one-night thing. I'm extremely paranoid about my health.

JESSE: I'm finding this very scary that you don't remember what happened.

[1] Caine, Michael. *Acting for Film: An Actor's Take on Movie Making*. Applause Books, 1997.
[2] Inside the Actors Studio, James Lipton, Bravo TV.

CELINE: You know what, I didn't write an entire book, but I kept a journal and I wrote the whole night in it. That's what I meant by you idealizing the night.

JESSE: [*a bit louder*] I even remember the brand of condom I used.

CELEINE: That's disgusting.

Walking by are an older couple with three kids. They look back, a bit shocked.

JESSE: No it isn't.

CELINE: All right, when I get home, I'll check my journal from '94, but I know I'm right.

A beat.

Wait a minute. Was it in the cemetery?

JESSE: Noooo. We visited the cemetery during the day. It was in the park, very late at night.

CELINE: Wait a minute.

JESSE: Was it that forgettable? You don't remember, in the park?

CELINE: Wait a minute, I think you might be right.

JESSE: You're messing with me.

In this scene, Celine does more of the talking than Jesse, so it's acutely important for Jesse to keep his inner monologue going. If his inner monologue is 'I can't believe this. She doesn't remember having sex with me. I can't believe this. She doesn't remember having sex with me. I can't believe this. She doesn't remember having sex with me', then he's probably giving a pretty boring performance. Just as the choices on line readings are important, so are the choices on inner monologue and subtext, and the same rules apply. The camera loves contrast and change. The camera loves discovery. So the actor playing Jesse needs to spin not only an active but also a varied inner monologue. Some of the different thoughts winding around in his head could be:

— *I know we had sex and I'm undressing you with my eyes right now.*

— *Was I that awful in bed that you don't remember?*

— *Maybe we really didn't have sex and I just imagined it.*

— *You must be kidding!*

Then finally . . .

— *Thank God she remembers!*

If these types of varied thoughts are revolving, his performance will live and breathe.

If thinking in character isn't effective for you then do whatever works. Dustin Hoffman says, 'The method is your method'.[3] Billy Bob Thornton, while performing in *The Man Who Wasn't There*, spent a lot of time on screen without uttering a word. When asked what he was thinking about in his reaction shots, he glibly replied that he was thinking a lot about James Gandolfini's shoes.[4] I'm also reminded of Wim Wender's film *Wings of Desire*, in which angels overheard the inner thoughts of humankind. While trailing actor Peter Falk on a film set in Berlin they picked up on him thinking, 'I wonder what I'll have for dinner. Maybe some spaghetti with marinara sauce'. Nobody really cares what your process is. Your method, whether it be thinking the character's thoughts or thinking about lunch, is what works for you. A solid bet is to activate the face and the eyes with a charged and changing inner monologue. Dead face is deadly.

Things to remember from this chapter

* Possess an inner monologue

* An inner monologue is the antidote to both dead face and overacting

* The camera loves contrast and discovery

* Do whatever works for you to create an active and alive performance where the wheels in the head are turning

---

[3] Inside the Actors Studio, James Lipton, Bravo TV.
[4] Ibid.

7 Commit to the scene — not the lines in the scene

What happens in the scene? What does the character want? It is more important to nail *what happens* in the scene, than to perform a perfectly memorized line reading. I have seen actors who become so obsessed with flawlessly reciting the lines that they miss the point of the scene. It is not interesting to watch an actor, without a script in his hand, struggle to recall lines. Remember that the casting is not a memory test. The more familiar you are with the text, the easier it will be to act, but keeping the script in hand is accepted in the UK and US. We all know how easily the lines flow when you're rehearsing it in your bedroom, but somehow they all fall out of your head when you're at the casting. Holding the sides is a kind of security blanket and it reminds us that this is not a finished performance, it's a work in progress.

If you get a word wrong, don't point out your mistake; mistakes can result in fresh discovery. Too many times, I have seen actors want to stop the scene and repeat it merely because they fluffed a line. You need to behave at the casting in the way you behave on set. Cover and continue. It took the crew hours to set up the shot, so you shouldn't make them stop the reel for a line error. The editor can cut around it. Part of what we're testing in the casting is your ability to concentrate and get through the scene. Therefore stay in the scene, even if your pants are on fire, until you hear 'cut'.

We are not interested that you say the lines perfectly. We're interested in what you bring to the role. We want to see your interpretation, your energy, your choices, your dynamic. Don't worry about pronunciation. When we were casting *Dune*, actors had to stumble over words like 'Ibn Qirtaiba' and 'Ikhut-Eigh' — language specific to Frank Herbert's sci-fi world. At the castings, it was a source of stress for the actors, but we didn't care about it. We knew that they would pick it up on set where we had a dialogue coach. If you mess up a few lines, you will be forgiven if you are playing the character's actions and objectives. Pull us into the story and it might not even matter what words are coming from your mouth.

In a comedy, committing to the scene means telling the jokes properly. In this case, if you don't get the wording right on a punch line, the joke doesn't work. In a comedic scene, your job is to figure out the jokes and tell them. A carefully planned joke doesn't work with lots of 'umm's and 'err's. It needs to be told concisely.

Sometimes the writer is at the casting, if they are, get it right. You want to do as much justice to the script as you can. The casting is generally not the time to intentionally change the text. Casting director Jane Jenkins notes, 'I tend to get

Oooops! Can I try that again?

annoyed when actors make wholesale changes to the script while reading for the director — simply improvising their own dialogue, changing the rhythm that the writer has carefully constructed. This is especially problematic — not to mention insulting — when the director is also the writer.'[1]

Things to remember from this chapter

* Memorize the lines if you wish, but more importantly memorize what is important in the scene

* Casters are more interested in what you bring to the role than your perfect recitation of the lines

* Keep the scene going even if you do fluff a line

[1] Hirshenson, Janet and Jenkins, Jane with Kranz, Rachel. *A Star is Found: Our Adventures Casting Some of Hollywood's Biggest Movies.* Harvest Books, Harcourt, Inc., San Diego, 2006.

8 Stake a claim, take a risk

> *Actors who come in and own the part are the people we have confidence in. They're the ones we're happy to present to a director, because they'll make us look good.* [1]
>
> Janet Hirshenson, Casting Director

This is your time. Remember you are entitled to be at that casting. You were invited and you deserve to be there. Take your time, own the space, and stake a claim to the role. The actors who are humble and enter with the attitude of, 'You, Oh Great Director, have granted me this favor of your time, so I, little actor, will hurry', are not the ones who get cast. Directors feel comfortable with self-possessed actors, who are confident in their abilities. Ask questions if you have any, and take a beat before you start the scene to focus yourself.

Staking a claim means being physically and psychically prepared. Do whatever you need to do to warm up beforehand. No one will warm you up at the audition. I'm shocked when I see an actor reading a newspaper in reception before performing an unprepared audition.

Sometimes actors want to walk in the door already in character. This is one approach but you have to be ready because some casting directors like to chat first. If this is your case, inform the receptionist that you're ready to go right into it so that he can tell the auditors that you want to work that way. Most casting directors will respect this approach.

---

[1] Hirshenson, Janet and Jenkins, Jane with Kranz, Rachel. *A Star is Found: Our Adventures Casting Some of Hollywood's Biggest Movies.* Harvest Books, Harcourt, Inc., San Diego, 2006.

You're not there to fetch the director's slippers

The actor who gets cast is the actor who commands the room and boldly squares off with the material. When actor Petr Vanek read for the role of Felipe the bellboy in *Last Holiday*, he had a scene in which Georgia (Queen Latifah's character) asks him, 'Did I over-tip you?' The scripted reply is yes. Instead he replied no (with a sneaky sparkle in his eye, like he didn't want to return the super big tip) and director Wayne Wang gave a hearty laugh. Petr was commanding the scene and the attention of everyone in the room. He wasn't in fact playing the lines, he made another choice, but he made it work with the scene. No one cared that he read the wrong line because he owned the scene, and was claiming the role. He got it.

Producer Frank Marshall discusses this concept in an interview about *The Sixth Sense*.[2] For the disturbed boy's mother, director M. Night Shyamalan wanted an actor with an authentic Philadelphian accent, but he ended up casting an Australian. 'There's a moment when an actor comes in they claim the role,' said Marshall. 'And Toni Collette did that . . . she just got it. She knocked us out.'

Jane Jenkins has a similar observation about Sophie Tatou auditioning for *The Da Vinci Code*. She came to the meeting as if she was coming to a rehearsal:

[2] *The Sixth Sense*. Back material. DVD. The Kennedy Marshall Company. Spyglass Entertainment.

'We could see . . . that this was the first actress who had shown up without an entire vision of the character that she was ready to present; instead, she had allowed her performance to unfold, and Tom [Hanks] had given her the pace to do that. But she found an approach that worked, he matched her energy — and the two of them began to create a powerful chemistry . . . she had three films under her belt . . . and was doing another film . . . and she felt no need to show us how good she was. Instead, she simply worked on the character the way an actress, does. Trying different things, allowing the character to inhabit her, letting things take their own instinctive course. She didn't need to impress us — and as a result, she could take bigger risks.'[3]

Approach the process as if you already have the role. Come into the audition as if to rehearse. That's what the movie stars do. At a rehearsal, you can take risks and play with the material.

> *You're only as good as the chance that you take.*
>
> Al Pacino, Actor

There are far too many actors who play it safe. Don't be afraid to take the scene somewhere. Remember that we're seeing hundreds of auditions. There will be many actors who can technically act the scene but what do they bring to it? A good place to take risks is in the places where the scene changes. Dare to hit the transitions. Most scenes have a turning point, a place where the scene hinges or the dynamic changes. The scene needs to go from A to Z, not A to B. The camera loves contrast and change.

I went to the opera to see Mozart's *The Marriage of Figaro*. The singer who sang the famous 'Aprite un po' aria performed this biting number about the treachery of women with the passion of a plumber fixing a drain. He sang it perfectly but I felt like falling asleep. He had a lovely, trained operatic voice and he hit every note with a measured expertise, but there was no love in it. Dare to climb out on a limb, to jump and to soar.

---

[3] Hirshenson, Janet and Jenkins, Jane with Kranz, Rachel. *A Star is Found: Our Adventures Casting Some of Hollywood's Biggest Movies*. Harvest Books, Harcourt, Inc., San Diego, 2006.

Things to remember from this chapter

❋ Claim the role

❋ Warm yourself up before you step through the door

❋ Play the scene like you've already got the role and you're at the first rehearsal

❋ Take a risk; too many actors play it safe

❋ The camera loves contrast, discovery and change

9 Tell the story

For as many times as it is appropriate to take a risk, there are equally as many times when it's appropriate to simply tell the story. While casting a TV series for guest roles, I noticed that whenever actors took a risk and did something interesting, the director would say that they were overacting. This is when story telling comes in. The director wants you to mesh into his story, not pop out. David Mamet, defending the position of the writer, wants an 'uninflected performance' from the actor. In other words, he doesn't want the performer to mess up his text by acting too much. Trust that you are expressing enough, and that the chemistry of your persona, merging with the objective of the character, will tell the story. You don't have to do handstands for the role.

Remember that you are only telling one piece of the story. Film is ultimately a director's art, with him coordinating the elements — set, costume, sound, lighting design — and arranging them with an editor. These combined elements tell the story. Sergei Eisenstein was an early twentieth century Russian director who originated the idea of a montage. He proved that the actor's performance by itself has no efficacy without the context of the film. He conducted an experiment in which he filmed an actor doing different reaction shots. First he instructed the actor to react is if he had just been brought a bowl of soup after not having eaten for a week. Then in a separate scene, he directed him to react as a recently released prisoner, seeing birds in the sky for the first time in years. When the audience viewed the scenes, of course they couldn't tell what the actor was experiencing, proving that the acting alone cannot show thought — editing must. It's the scenes that are interspersed with the actor's reactions that tell the story. Let the text and your voice carry the scene. Read the lines. Keep it simple.

Things to remember from this chapter

✳ Remember that you are a story teller

✳ Trust your uninflected performance, combined with objective and text, will tell the story

✳ Film is a director's medium. You don't have to tell the entire story yourself, just a small piece of it

Listen

No man ever listened himself out of a job.

Calvin Coolidge, 30th President of the USA

You may talk your way into a corner but you can never listen too much. There are two types of listening that must take place. The first is for the *actor* to listen and respond to the director's notes. The second is that the *character* must listen and react in the moment to the actor who is reading the other part. He is your opponent in a tennis game and if you don't listen, you don't know where the ball is.

One unfortunate but common mistake is when an actor speaks very animatedly but listens like a zombie, simply waiting for the other actor to finish his line, or even worse anticipating what the other will say. The camera is unforgiving of this error. If you haven't had much time with the text, the temptation is to read the other character's lines instead of *listening* to them. Keep your finger on the text and listen to the reader, then find your line again. It's OK if there is a slight delay. Actors who don't listen are often text obsessed, so afraid of dropping a line that they just stare at the script. It's more important to listen and to react to the other character than it is to get the line exactly correct.

You might get a really poor partner at the casting. Casting directors have been known to play the other role themselves, and there's no vouching for acting talent in those situations. Sometimes they hire a professional actor to read but there is no guarantee that they will give energy or a good performance. They might even have been instructed to read deadpan so as not to influence you.

That is something you have to work with. Even on set, you might end up playing with lousy talent or you might be delivering your lines to the assistant director's fist.

The next time you watch a film, observe how many times the camera is on the actor who is listening. It's there a lot. Director and teacher Patrick Tucker notes that, 'The viewer does not want to know how the [speaking] person feels about something she has just said, they want to know what the other person feels about it; this is the unknown in the scene'.[2] Listening is interesting. Listening also entails reacting, internally if there are no lines, and externally if there is a line. You may be forming your answer in your head half way into the other actor's speech. Listen with your eyes. Listening and reacting in character is at the heart of effective screen acting.

In the CBS TV film, *Hitler: The Rise of Evil*, we cast the late Patricia Netzer as Sophie Gerlich almost entirely because of her listening skills. Patricia prepared a self-taped scene and sent it to us. What sold the producer most was the part of her audition where she simply put the camera on herself and listened, silently reacting to a conversation between her husband and Hitler. The director knew that with this actor on set he would always have a place to put the camera. If you are a good listener, you will get more screen time. In the words of the Greek philosopher Plutarch, 'Know how to listen, and you will profit even from those who talk badly'.

Things to remember from this chapter

✴ Listen to the director's notes

✴ Listen to the other character in the scene

✴ The camera loves a good listener

✴ Your reaction to the other actor is as important as your line delivery

---

[1] Tucker, Patrick. *Secrets of Screen Acting.* Theatre Arts Books, Routledge, 2003.

11 Wag your tail

An actor comes home to find his wife, bruised and badly beaten. He huddles down to his crying spouse and desperately demands, 'Who did this to you? I'll kill him.'

'It was . . .' she weakly tries to answer.

'Was it the mail man?' he interrupts, 'I always thought he was suspicious.'

'No, no . . .' she stammers, trying to find the words.

'Was it the gardener? That swine!'

'No, no . . . it was your agent.'

'My agent stopped by?' he asks hopefully.

Don't be an actor who sits and waits by the phone for your agent to call. This is a miserable way to live. If the phone isn't ringing, staring at it won't help. Actors need to be proactive. One of my teachers used to say, 'It's a poor dog who can't wag his own tail'. So get out there and wag your tail.

Once an actor complained to me that he wasn't succeeding because casting directors ignored him. He said, 'The casting directors have control over my career and whether I make it or not'. This is absolutely not true. Take the power back. You are the only one who is in charge of whether you succeed or not.

This is the most valuable advice that I can give actors. Make your own work. If no one is casting you, if there is no one making a film or play with a role that is right for you, then make one for yourself. Write a play about you, directed by you, produced by you, with you in mind. Create the perfect role for yourself. If you don't like to write, then find material. There are plenty of good plays out there. When you are doing theatre, 'push yourself and work with good people', advises casting director Meg Liberman. You will learn from your co-stars. Not only are you attracting possible agents and casters, you are also honing your skills and getting better with each performance.

Many cities have fringe festivals. If yours doesn't, then start one. Fringe festivals are full of that sizzling energy created by hundreds of talented actors who are desperate to work. These actors are seizing the moment, practicing their craft. As the nineteenth century playwright, Friedrich Schiller said, '. . . he who has lived the best of his own age will live for many ages to come'. It is these performances that will burn themselves into the minds of viewers, not just the big blockbuster films. Stars who got their start at the Edinburgh Fringe Festival, for example, include Jude Law, Gerard Butler, Hugh Grant, Ricky Gervais and Rachel Weisz. There was a time when these actors weren't famous but they didn't get noticed by sitting at home.

Steven Berkoff confesses that he composed his now famous adaptation of Franz Kafka's story *Metamorphosis* when he was out of work and sick of waiting for the phone to ring. *Metamorphosis* was nothing more than a talent vehicle for Berkoff — playing a cockroach of all things. Now Berkoff can languidly wait by the phone. This time, in addition to getting acting offers, he's waiting for his agent to call and report on the royalties he earns when the play is produced as a star vehicle for other actors, like, for example, Mikhail Baryshnikov. If you create a good role, other actors will want to play it too.

If your phone isn't ringing with film offers, then take the reigns into your own hands, and make a film yourself. You don't need millions to make a film — all you need is a camera (a simple digital video camera will do), a computer with an editing program, and a lot of ideas, energy and enthusiasm. Choose something that matters to you and find your voice to express it through film.

There are independent film festivals bursting out of every city. If no one accepts your film, then you can pop it on YouTube. There are even on— line film festivals. The internet bars no one from promoting their work. Unknown actors are able to attract agents and auditions for top notch roles when they produce good online work. At time of print, Etta Divine provides an excellent example of self-promotion with her online series that starts with *Girl's Night Out.* She created a role for herself, shot on a skeleton budget attracting agents, auditions and thousands of online viewers through a YouTube posting.

The film *Good Will Hunting* launched the careers of Matt Damon and Ben Affleck, and it was written by ... guess who? Matt Damon and Ben Affleck. Some of the world's best drama has come from actors who wrote material for themselves to perform; don't forget William Shakespeare was an actor.

Vin Diesel didn't know that he was on course for action hero super-stardom when he made his own film, *Multi-Facial* in 1994. The film, about multiculturalism and identity, was close to his heart. He made the film because he had a passion to express himself. That $3,000 film was accepted for the Cannes Film Festival in 1995, eventually catching the attention of Steven Spielberg, who offered him a role in *Saving Private Ryan*. Other actors who started by writing their own .material include Owen Wilson, Ben Stiller, Steve Martin, Tina Fey, and Emma Thompson.

If you feel that producing or writing aren't for you, then team up with someone else. Actor and producer Colleen Camp advises actors to 'align with people you think are talented, and be an entrepreneur. Write for yourself, write for someone else and get them to write for you'. Colleen is an excellent example. After many years as a jobbing actor, she started her own production company and has produced nine films.

If you're out there doing it, you might not even have time to answer the phone when we call you. When I was casting *Everything is Illuminated*, we needed an actor to play a comic Hitler. Pip Utton was touring a one-man show called *Adolph*. Utton had written the play and was playing the title role. He caught my attention from his good reviews of playing the Führer at the Edinburgh Fringe Festival. Ironically, he wasn't available because he was too busy touring his show.

When you're doing a play, you've got a product that you can invite casting directors and agents to come see. Collect reviews from your play and you've got material to send out and post on your website. If it's a short film, you can send the whole film, or edited scenes of your best work can go on a show reel and can be uploaded to your website as well.

Take David Mamet's advice: 'If you have character, your work will have character. The character to do exercises every day over the years creates the strength of character to form your own theatre rather than go to Hollywood'.[1] You heard Mr. Mamet; make your own Hollywood!

> *You are your business. You have to do everything you can to support your business. Your agent can't teach you the juggling skills, riding or singing or whatever. They can get you through the door and can say 'I've got an actor who can play the oboe', but they can't play it for you; you have to do everything to make you, your business, as wide ranging as possible. And I would also say if you're not working, please don't sit around being out of work. Spend time with children or do something else so that when you come to a meeting, you're not thinking, 'God, I haven't worked in six months', but you can say, 'I took six months off because I wanted to help handicapped children'; suddenly you become very interesting.*
>
> Emma Style, Casting Director, UK

Things to remember from this chapter

❋ Wagging your own tail means don't be modest, learn to promote yourself

❋ Don't sit by the phone giving all the power to casting directors

❋ Make a film or play starring yourself

❋ Get active in the theatre

---

[1] Mamet, David. *True and False: Heresy and Common Sense for the Actor.* Vintage Books, USA, Random House, New York, 1999.

Part 2

The nuts and bolts of casting

12 FAQs about auditioning and casting

> *Learn the rules so that you know how to break them properly.*
>
> The Dalai Lama

Here are the rules. The trick is figuring out when to break them. While I answer these frequently asked questions, there are no formulas for the acting trade.

What can I expect at a film or TV casting?

Be prepared to expect almost anything and roll with it. Usually for film or TV casting you can expect there to be a camera. There might be several people in the room, or just the casting director and the camera. If it's a large 'cattle' call, they may give you a number before you go into the studio. Usually you need to hold the number under your chin while they take a photo for identification. Often you will be asked to stand neutrally in front of camera, and turn for both profiles before you start reading. (Yes, like in jail, and they've heard that joke before.) For a commercial they will want you to display your hands and a toothy smile, but don't offer this in a film casting. (It will tell us that you do mostly commercials.)

Some casting directors may surprise you by handing you another role or asking you to improvise a scene that you know nothing about. Each director has a different approach. Terrence Malick, for example, does improvisations with his actors then builds the roles around them. One of my students said that he was completely thrown when auditioners asked him to speak his lines in Polish.

Though he had a Polish name, he didn't speak Polish, so they told him to make up a gibberish Polish language.

Often you are expected to introduce yourself in front of camera, for the benefit of the director. This means making a simple introduction: state your name, agency, perhaps height and mention a few of your best projects. Do not mention your age. Your playing range is all that matters.

The introduction seems to be the hardest part of the audition for some actors. They can't wait to transform themselves into a character but they feel uncomfortable just being themselves for a few moments. Yet to a director this might be the most interesting moment. It's vitally important that you reveal your own personality. *You* are the product and *you* are really the most interesting thing from our side of the camera. 'The actors are my teachers', said director Stephen Frears about *My Beautiful Launderette*. He took all of his cues from them since he knew very little about India when he started the film.

If the director is at the audition, he may ask you to say a little about yourself or ask what you have been doing recently. As casting director John Hubbard noted in a symposium I moderated, 'That doesn't mean he's actually interested, so don't go on all day'. It's OK to plan what you'll say in this situation. If you say you love hang glide and you've been taking advantage of the great weather to do that lately it shows a passion and is something unusual for the director to remember. Say if you've just thrown a birthday party for your adorable three year old daughter; it introduces you not just as an actor, but also as a mother or a dad.

Leave problems outside the casting room door. Saying you've not been doing much, just staying in doing housework doesn't give a very good impression. The director doesn't want to work with someone who doesn't even take an interest in her own life. If the director asks you what projects you've worked on lately, remember that he doesn't want to hear your entire resume. Briefly summarize the projects that showcase you well. 'I've just been working with X actor in a BBC series. It was really fun; we got to shoot in Cornwall. Have you ever been there?' Remember to spin it in the most positive way. Some actors don't feel adequate and they demote themselves. Turn 'I was in *Lord of the Rings* but it was a really small role,' into 'I've just worked on *Lord of the Rings*. It was a fantastic opportunity to work with Peter Jackson'.

On *Van Helsing*, I introduced an actor to the London casting director, Priscilla John, for the role of Dracula. While she was interviewing him, he continually focused on the negative saying things like, 'Well, I stopped working in that theatre as I didn't get along with the director'. Never mention negative work relationships at an interview. Remember that it is a job audition and we want to work with people who will cooperate. Needless to say, he wasn't cast.

What if I haven't worked much or I haven't worked in a long time?

Being unknown can be a great asset because it means that some agent or casting director can claim that they 'discovered' you. Great movie stars have been discovered at times when directors were searching for unknowns. When I was casting *Alien Vs. Predator*, I asked director Paul Anderson if we were casting any stars and he said, 'We have two stars. Alien and Predator'. When Steven Spielberg was casting *Jaws*, he said, 'I wanted somewhat anonymous actors to be in it so you would believe this was happening to people like you and me. Stars bring a lot of memories along with them, and those memories can sometimes, at least in the first ten minutes of the movie, corrupt the story'.[1]

Some actors don't break through until later in their careers. Naomi Watts landed the lead in *King Kong* when she was thirty-six. Casting director Priscilla John addressed the issue of the non-working actor in a casting symposium, 'There are plenty of actors who succeed in their thirties or forties, and you think, "I always knew he'd turn the corner even if he wasn't working much in his twenties, but he's coming into an interesting time." ' Casting director Maureen Duff sited the example of Eileen Essell, who has a successful acting career that she started when she was eighty!

When a director is interviewing you about your career, spin it your way. 'I haven't done much of anything, really. I'm just out of school,' can become 'I'm hitting the scene now. I just finished a really great course at X University', or 'I've been studying with a really exciting teacher, named Y.' Instead of 'I've only done an unpaid student film', try 'I've just finished working on a really exciting project about a teacher in the inner city; it was a great role for me'. Remember that the director probably knows that you're inexperienced. Bring your enthusiasm and your self with you.

---

[1] Biskind, Peter. *Easy Riders, Raging Bulls: How the Sex 'n' Drugs 'n' Rock 'n' Roll Generation Saved Hollywood.* Bloomsbury, 1998.

Who will be there?

This varies. Sometimes it's just the casting director or sometimes the director will be there too. Director Joe Wright, for example, sat in on every audition for *Charles II* for the BBC. In the US and at film auditions generally, this is less common at the first audition. Old hand casting director, Fred Roos (now a producer) explains that in the 1970s directors (including Francis Ford Coppola and George Lucas) frequently sat in on even the first meeting. Though that's uncommon in these days, be prepared for anything.

If it's a callback, you're likely to have the director, and if it's TV, the producer may come as well. If it's US network TV, your third callback is likely to be a test option deal at which point you read for the studio. Once you get past that point, you read for the network. Meg Liberman, who has cast numerous US network series, advises actors in these callbacks to 'replicate the [first] audition', unless directed otherwise.

The important thing is to do the research, not only on your role and the project but on who will be at the casting. Ask or have your agent find out for you. Know who you're meeting and what their credits are. See some of their work if possible. It gives you an idea of their style and a topic of conversation. When I was working on *Wanted*, Timur Bekmambetov took notice of the actors who introduced themselves by mentioning that they really liked his film, *Night Watch*.

Get to know who the casting director is, their name, and what they look like. This sounds obvious but it doesn't occur to a lot of actors. We may meet an actor in a casting on a Monday but in a café on Tuesday they have no idea who we are. We meet thousands of actors, so why is it that we remember them better than they remember us? Is it because they're so nervous or pre-occupied that they don't see who is in the room with them? Sheila Jaffe who casts *The Sopranos* told me that she's gone to the wrap parties where actors she cast didn't recognize her. Remember the hand that feeds you. Keep up with casting directors and their careers.

> When I go to an audition for a film (we go to auditions too, we don't have to do a piece but I do have to wear a tie and speak in a nice voice), I always try to find out something about the people I'm meeting. I will meet them and say something like, '1

liked that film you did'. You're immediately getting in touch with them. We once met with Robert Altman and just as he was leaving, Ros said, 'I loved the little boy you cast in Popeye'. *Altman said, 'Oh my God, that was my grandson'. And he was so touched that she remembered something like that.*

John Hubbard, Casting Director, London

What happens at callbacks?

Great you got a callback! This means that after your initial casting, you've been asked to return. The casting director wants to work with you some more. You may be meeting the director and he might have invited other actors to see who plays well with whom. In rare cases, you may even read with the star. Casting director Jane Jenkins in her book *A Star is Found* discusses how she called in actors for a very small role to 'read' with Russell Crowe for *A Beautiful Mind*. I put read in quotes since this character didn't even speak, she just slaps him when he makes an awkward pass at her.

To prepare for a callback, know the lines. Callbacks tend to make actors even more edgy as they are that much closer to the role. Some actors do a wonderful first audition but bomb the callback. The mistake is that they over-prepare, making it impossible to receive direction and play with the role and their choices. Actors also tend to think they need to prove their acting abilities, so show off, do too much or make that fatal mistake of judging the character. Keep it simple. Know the character, make specific choices and let it flow.

At callbacks, we're looking at the alchemy of the cast and how they fit together. If you've made it to the callback stage, you don't have to prove yourself. We already think you're a good actor. Often we're assessing your chemistry with another actor or simply your personal chemistry and how it meshes with the role. This is not something that you can push: either it's there or it's not. My yoga teacher advises, 'The more you relax, the further you'll stretch'. It works at a callback audition too.

Should I get university training?

If you get accepted into Julliard or LAMBA or any other top drama school you've got a great start to your career. These top institutions, by name alone, immediately impress and lead to invaluable work contacts. Casting director Maureen Duff regards them as a kind of 'insurance policy if you don't know the actor'. Top drama schools, however, are not the exclusive formula to success. In show business there is no prescribed trajectory.

If you want a liberal arts education, then by all means earn one. This degree could include a specialism in theatre or film. A liberal arts degree is an excellent foundation for acting because history, science, and literature are all important when making decisions for building a character. In terms of the real world of show business, however, having a BA or Bachelor of Fine Arts (BFA) on your CV doesn't count for much. It's about what you can do. I've never regretted my education but, for the jobs I've had in entertainment, no employer has ever bothered about my diplomas. I learned on the job. Actors learn on the job too. While I heartily encourage actors to get as much quality training as possible, it does not have to be in a university setting. There are many excellent training courses and teachers who don't necessarily offer a degree. Natalie Portman famously said, 'I'm going to college. I don't care if it ruins my career. I'd rather be smart than a movie star'. (She is both.) If an actor has no knowledge or life experience than there is very little on which to build.

> *Some young people come in with this huge dossier of certificates and I don't even open the book. It's about what is in front of me and what they are capable of. I do think that in terms of education, actors should be well informed, should read books, be aware of the world, go to theatre, go to films, be aware of the types of characters that are being cast ... that's the type of education that's important for acting. It's not diplomas or universities. It's get on the stage and act.*
>
> John Hubbard, Casting Director, London

I'm a trained actor. Must I keep training even after I have completed my degree work?

Yes. Leonardo DiCaprio, Nicole Kidman, and Helen Hunt all have acting coaches. If you think you're a better actor than they are, then skip it. Training is on-going for actors. Take courses and master classes in improvisation, stand-up, Meisner technique, Viewpoints, Shakespearean verse, stage combat, film acting, scene study, audition technique, clowning and physical theatre whenever you can. Even if musical theatre isn't your specialty make sure that you're studying voice and dance as well. Being physically fit is important. It's part of keeping the instrument tuned. Acting is physical.

Should I lie about my age?

For some reason actors have this bizarre idea that they should always claim to be younger than their actual age, as if the only roles available are for people under thirty. On the contrary, once I was casting a commercial for which we needed thirty-something women and a thirty five year old actor announced that she was twenty-nine. The director crossed her off his list until I told him later that she was lying. The only thing that matters is your playing range. By announcing your age (your correct age or a fantasy age) you limit your options. Therefore, on your CV list only your playing range (20–30, for example). The playing range should be believable and probably within ten to fifteen years of your true age.

In the internet age, it's impossible to hide your age anyway. Once your age is reported to IMDB, it's impossible to remove it. Stick to the age range when face to face with a director though, since he is rarely staring into his computer while interviewing you. In some cases, age range actually has nothing to do with your actual age. A prematurely bald actor, for example, often plays roles older than himself. Let the casting director lie for you if necessary. Casting director Leo Davis confesses that she regularly lies to directors about age on actors' behalf.

One of the famous examples of an actor playing against his true age is Dustin Hoffman, who played the eighteen year-old Benjamin Braddock in *The Graduate*. He was thirty playing opposite Anne Bancroft, only five years his senior, who was meant to be his mother's age. Casting history is full of these examples, so keep your options open.

What do I wear?

The important rule is to wear something that flatters, without upstaging. Casting director Anja Dihrberg notes that, 'If the costume becomes more important than the acting, then we have a problem'. Neutral, solid colors work well. No stripes, no loud colors, nor white — it reflects the light. Be careful about what jewelry you choose. We want to cast you, not your earrings. Any hats are bad, as are t-shirts with writing.

Sometimes women feel the need to sex themselves up at castings. (See Beatrice Kruger's comments about this in the Chapter 21.) While I would advise anyone to play their assets, remember that you want them to notice your acting not your bust line. If it's a particularly sexy role, however, then go for it. For *Van Helsing*, we had a role called 'buxom bar maid', where we encouraged candidates for this role to let it shine. 'There's nothing wrong with wearing a tight t-shirt if the role requires muscle definition,' notes talent manager, Derek Power. I generally want to see an actor's waist, whether it is big or small.

Some actors are considered too 'contemporary looking' to play in a period film. A tanned actor who looks great jumping off a surf board in one show, may not be convincing in a seventeenth century piece. For a period drama, it may be advisable for a man to grow a beard or whiskers (if there is time) before the casting. Women with dyed or streaked hair, flattened down with a hair straighteners are less likely to be cast for period roles as well. Don't flaunt a tattoo; it makes a problem for the make-up department.

For a callback it's advisable to wear the same outfit that you wore for the first audition. You will immediately be recognizable to the director. He short-listed you and he remembers you as the guy in the mauve t-shirt.

Should I dress as the character?

This is the million-dollar question and it's hotly debated. Most casting directors are happy when an actor suggests the costume somehow. Although you're theoretically auditioning for creative people, don't count on them having a well-developed imagination. Make it easy for them. It's hard for them to imagine you as an investment banker if you're wearing a tie-dye t-shirt. Help them out and wear a suit. Some actors come prepared with a few different clothing options. Be time efficient and make sure you can slip them on and off quickly. Generally, casting directors find it absurd when actors go overboard with costumes. You don't have to rent a partlet if you're up for an Elizabethan era piece. Here are two examples of casting director comments, from a symposium:

John Hubbard: I knew an English production company and they went to LA to cast for this commercial and all the actors turned up as Batman. About an hour later the producer turned around and said to the casting director, 'Why are they all dressed as Batman? We're casting a batman'. I think what you have to do is something that suggests the character, subtly.

Maureen Duff: I was casting *Tom Brown's School Days* and there was one particular actor who didn't have an agent but kept calling and was desperate to read so we finally let him, and he came in with a nineteenth century costume. Silver cane and hat and everything and he screamed at the top of his lungs — an awful reading. As soon as he left the room we all just burst out laughing. But he'd forgotten his silver cane so he had to come back . . .

There are simple things that actors do to subtly alter their dress, without turning heads on the bus en route to auditions. A good choice for period drama is wearing an accessory or hairdo that suggests that era. A suit coat for women in a 1940s piece or a waistcoat for men can go a long way. Be dressed and ready when they call your name. No casting director wants to wait while you change clothes.

Actor Colleen Camp provides a wonderful exception to the no elaborate costumes rule. She was competing against top actors, like Madonna and Demi Moore, for the role of Yvette in *Clue.* At the callback, Colleen came bouncing in wearing a French maid's costume and she played the costume so well that from that moment on the casting team couldn't imagine anyone else in the role.

Should I wear make-up?

It's a good idea to even out your skin tone with a light covering of foundation. The camera detects all. Think about the specific role and what makes sense cosmetically. When we were casting vampires on *Blade II*, Andrea Miltner, who played the first vampire of the film, came to her audition with ghost white foundation and dark red lips. It helped us to see her as a vampire and she was cast. Sometimes I specifically ask actors not to wear make-up if we're looking for an unpolished look. The things you normally try to hide might be the things that get you cast. When I was acting, a director said to me, 'I want to use the dark circles under your eyes for this role'. Sometimes women overdo their eye make-up. Liner and mascara are designed to accentuate but too much eye make-up upstages. Bette Davis advised that if you want to bring out your eyes, wear brown eyeliner, not black. If your make-up is too thick, you're drawing attention to your liner, not your eyes. Bette Davis, famous for her eyes, should know.

What if I don't know anything about the film?

It's difficult to act in a vacuum. Research the project as much as you can in advance. You can request a copy of the script but sometimes a production won't let it out of the office. Ask if you can come early to the audition and read the script in the waiting room. If you're auditioning for a Bond film or a Woody Allen script, the chances are you won't see the screenplay until after you get the job, and maybe not even then. When the production provides you with the script, read it! There is nothing that turns a director off more than a missed opportunity. Casting directors don't want to hear stories about your printer breaking down.

If you aren't given the option to read the script, then remember that it's an even playing field for all competing actors. A synopsis is usually provided. Most of the information that you need is in the sides. Ask and answer the most important questions: Who am I? Where am I? Who am I talking to? What do I want? What are the stakes? If you're not sure, then decide anyway.

Research demonstrates interest. Look up the project on IMDB.com and other websites to see what you can learn. If the piece is based on real life events or history, know the facts. The more you know, the better you'll perform and the better impression you'll make. When I had my interview for *Shanghai Knights*, I made sure that I saw *Shanghai Days* first, so I could have an intelligent conversation with the director about the style of the film.

> *I went to the casting initially knowing that there were hundreds of girls going up for it. I just read the scene, and I had no idea who she was, what the character was doing, the title of the*

script, nothing. It was very, very secretive. Two weeks later I got a call saying 'Woody wants to meet you Monday morning. Will you go over to New York?' recalls actor Haley Atwell in an interview with The Times. *Subsequently, she got the lead in Woody Allen's* Cassandra's Dream, *without knowing a darn thing.*

Where do I look? Do I look at the camera?

Film generally follows the dictums of Realism, the concept of removing the fourth wall of a room. Just as actors in a Realist play do not look at the audience, we rarely see actors looking directly at camera in film. The performer is not supposed to be aware that she is being photographed so why would she be looking into camera? Unless specifically required, it is better to look next to the lens. Often the reader is positioned there anyway. If the reader is sitting in a place that is disadvantageous, then choose a spot next to the lens. You don't need to maintain eye contact with the reader. Which is your good side? You should know this if you want to be a film actor. Figure out which side of your face photographs better and play to that side. Bear in mind that you don't have to fixate on one focal point for the entire reading, but be as generous with your eyes as possible.

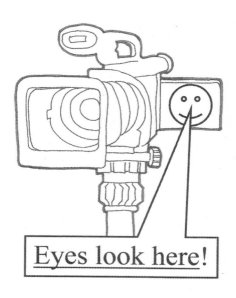

Eyes look here!

Screen acting is in the eyes so we must see them. During the actual filming, the director shoots a scene in all sorts of ways. The actor might be crouched down low, in semi-darkness, or the director may shoot over an actor's shoulder to get a point of view (PoV) shot. Let the director make these artistic decisions when she's shooting the film. When you're at a casting, however, the goal is to show yourself. That means uncreative blocking; play to camera and find a focal point right next to the lens.

When referring to or seeing something off camera, place it near the camera lens. Often actors choose a focal point that is on the floor (wrong! your eyes go down) or way off to the side (wrong! Then we don't see your eyes at all but only your profile) or even behind them (great if you want us to see the back of your head).

Work out who you're talking to and where they are. Make these decisions before you go into the room. Orient yourself, check where the camera is and where the other characters are in relation to it. The scene doesn't have to make geographical sense; let the director worry about that later. Play towards camera and locate yourself in the scene. No one will hold your hand through this process.

Is it important to be word perfect or off book?

In Chapter 7 I say that it is more important to know the scene than the lines. I encourage actors to learn lines, but to hold the script as security so that the audition doesn't become a memory test. But there are differences of opinion about this:

Beatrice Kruger, Casting Director, Europe: 'I think that an actor has to be relaxed. And in order to be relaxed at the audition, it's best if he knows the lines so he can play with them and he is free. If he has to remember the lines, then he will look like someone who is remembering the lines, so that's an obstacle. If he's got something in his hands, he's always going to be looking down. So I think if you have the time, you're best off learning the lines because then you're free. If you don't know it, then you can't play with it.'

John Hubbard, Casting Director, London: 'Get off the page. When actors come in so prepared, I say, "Didn't you get the sides?" and they have it all in their head and that really impresses and gets you closer to the job.'

Michael Shurtleff, Broadway Casting Director: Memorization for an audition is a 'complete waste of time'.[2]

Lina Todd, Casting Director, New York: 'It is certainly not expected in American casting that you would have the sides memorized. The problem is [that actors who] improvise the lines makes some writer/directors crazy, and others are actually quite fine with it. I remember when Jeremy Davies was reading for me and he was off book except he was way off book and the director went insane. But then when I watched the tape he only really changed three words but the writer's every word was so specific that it was too much for him to handle. I do think that an actor is freer if they're not glued to the page, but it certainly isn't expected.'

Lucinda Syson, Casting Director, London: 'I had an actor who said he hadn't learned the lines on purpose. He had been to a workshop where some very famous workshop person had advised him. With feature films, we use video cameras and the director isn't there most of the time. And the most important thing is your eyes and if you keep looking down at the page, it breaks concentration. I'm not just being schooly . . . it's really practical matter of loosing concentration. Categorically learn it.'

My advice also goes against the 'dead letter perfect' dictum, emphasized at British training schools. While working with Ian Richardson on *From Hell*, he told me that he found the lines awkward, since although this Jack the Ripper story took place in Victorian London, it was written in an American cadence of speech. He felt, however, it was his professional obligation to make the lines work, as written, so that he did. There are times when actors change lines slightly to make them flow better and some writers and directors go along when the changes improve the product. I've been in castings when the writer actually took notes on the actor's mistakes, wondering if it sounded better with alternative wording. Other writers, as previously noted by Lina Todd, have a thermal nuclear meltdown when even one line is changed.

[2] Shurtleff, Michael. *Audition: Everything an Actor Needs to Know to Get the Part.* Walker and Company, New York, 1978.

No matter how much you prepare, however, you cannot anticipate how much the scene will change and evolve. It is the very nature of television drama that the text is more like a blueprint than a cemented structure. While acting in television mini-series, I've memorized pages of script only to have it re-written on the day. For both NBC's *Revelations* and ABC's *Anne Frank*, the writers were present on set and re-wrote the lines by hand, passing them to me on the back of a call sheet. If this happens to you at a casting or on set, don't let it throw you. If you memorized the scene, meaning the *happening* in the scene, and the character's objectives, the scene will run smoothly.

What about accents?

When an accent is required, you have to speak convincingly on the day of the casting. Otherwise the director won't believe that you can do it. Dialect CDs are available. Penny Dyer, for example, is a respected dialect coach who offers a range of voice products including *Access Accents*, published by Methuen Drama, a series of hour-long voice coaching sessions on CD developed for actors needing to have an accent at a moment's notice. Have at least a few different accents under your belt. If you're British, then standard American is important. Conversely Americans should learn RP (Received Pronunciation or Standard British). Concentrate first on the accents that will be the most useful to you. If you're a white actor, you probably won't ever be expected to speak in a Chinese accent (believe it or not I have actually seen this on a resume). Only list the accents that you really have mastered. Often actors think they can do accents well, when actually they sound like cartoons. Get your accent approved by either a native speaker or a dialect coach.

If your audition requires a new accent and you have the time then do whatever you need to learn it. Rent a film that uses that dialect or find a radio programme on the internet. If your audition is the following day and you just can't master the accent in time, then be honest. It's better to use your own accent and confess, 'I don't know the accent now, but I'm very happy to learn it'. Poor accents can ruin the audition, especially if you're concentrating only on the accent and nothing else. The dialect has to be second nature to you.

'In my jobs, I prefer you enter already in the accent. Don't wait for someone to say "now go into the Birmingham accent," ' says Ros Hubbard.

What about volume? Must I project my voice?

Actors who come in projecting give themselves away immediately — theatre actor. A famous story about Sir Ralph Richardson recounts that after his first screen performance the director complained, 'It was all right, Ralph, except that I could hear you'. Theatre actors must throw their voices to the stalls. In film it's important to play to the microphone. If you are speaking to someone who is only a few feet away, speak relatively quietly. If the mike is one meter away, then adjust your voice accordingly. Occasionally there is a separate mike, on its own tripod or even attached to your clothing. In these cases, keep your voice at normal levels. If you think the character would be whispering for some reason, then whisper. If your character is talking to a large crowd, then use the full strength of your voice.

Shall I follow the stage directions in the script?

Identify when the stage directions are important. For example in *The Bourne Identity* scene in Part 5, Bourne throws Marie a bag of money. This is the moment of discovery in the scene. Bourne offers her $10,000 to drive him to Paris. She doesn't want to let a stranger into her car until this crucial moment. She's broke. Ten thousand dollars changes her mind, so in that case, play the stage direction.

Generally, however, you should ignore the stage directions for two reasons. First the writer is often trying to direct the actors or tell the director how to direct the scene. When they insert adjectives like stunned, perplexed, hurt etc. in parenthesis, ignore them. They are result oriented directions that won't help you act the scene. Stick to the objective and stray from adjectives provided by the writer. Sometimes you will see punctuation that dictates a certain performance. A dash in the middle of a word usually means the character has more to say but is cut off. In these cases be prepared to have more to say in case the other actor or reader doesn't cut you off. Sometimes writers will capitalize an entire line, which seems to mean that they want you to scream. You're the actor, so you make the choices about the performance. Above all, make the scene work.

The second reason to ignore stage directions is that the writer might also be trying to tell the casting director how to do his job. Andy Pryor, who casts *Dr. Who* and many BBC TV shows, was embarrassed to call in actors for the role called

'Fat Bitch'. The role name was a way of describing the character as unpleasant, but there are many ways to devise this through the acting. What's more, you might get the side and think, 'but I'm not fat!' — or blond, or whatever. I've called thin actors in on 'fat' roles, simply because I thought they could act the role. The writer's description of physical attributes throws actors off so just ignore it! (My apologies to my writer friends.)

The audition is artificial. The way we shoot a scene at a casting may be entirely different from how it will be shot in production. If the scene takes place in a car, we don't go out to the parking lot and shoot in a car. A walking scene is hard to film without a dolly and grip department, so be prepared to say the lines standing in place. If there are stage directions like 'they kiss', then make the scene work without kissing the casting director or the reader. (If it were a callback with another actor, on the other hand, you probably would be expected to kiss your partner.) With punches or any kind of physical violence, you will not be expected to punch anyone, though I've seen actors punch their own palm to make an effect. If the stage directions read 'Anna cries' and if the tears come, fine. If not, then play the scene organically and make it work with your choices. If the director really insists on tears then he'll let you know. Above all, play to camera as much as possible even when it doesn't make scenic 'sense' to do so.

Can I move around in front of camera?

Yes. You're not a caged lion. It's professional to ask the size of the frame so you know how to calibrate your movement. If it's a close up then focus performance in the face and eyes, mindful not to pop out of frame. Bobbing from side to side will make viewers seasick. You may also choose to walk into frame or perform some simple blocking but if so, let the camera operator know, so he can follow you.

You won't be expected to do the more demanding actions, unless it's a stunt audition. When I was auditioning stuntmen for *Running Scared*, for example, they all came in and checked the strength of the wall before they threw themselves onto it. If you're on a horse, don't feel the need to simulate the movement of a horse. You'll just make a fool out of yourself. Casting director Priscilla John advises: 'Stage directions, as a lot of my directors will remind actors, are actually for studio executives who are not that bright and have to have everything set out, so that they can visualize everything, every single moment. Beware of these pitfalls and think for yourself. "What is this character in relation to me?" Don't get yourself in knots about stage directions. We are not in the park on horseback, we're in my office doing the scene, adapting this reading and it makes sense that the camera is there'.

Can I use props in a casting?

When you're battling aliens in outer space, don't forget your weapons! You can use props, as long as they don't upstage your performance. We want to be looking at you, not your toy soldier set. A mobile phone works brilliantly as a compass, a faser gun, and a walking talkie. The most successful props are simple things that will support your performance. Even your script can become a doctor's clipboard and your umbrella a sword. Most casting directors will not object to whatever props might enhance your performance. Sometimes props will be provided.

Some casting directors prefer miming since it eliminates the awkwardness of props, but miming can be uncomfortable. During auditions for *Everything is Illuminated* director Liev Schreiber said, 'I don't want actors to act with anything that's not there'. I assume that Liev hates to audition with mimed actions.

What if the person I'm reading with stinks?

They probably will stink. Your reader might be the casting director, who thinks she can act but actually can't, or it may be a bored assistant. Even if it's an actor, they may not give you the energy you want. You are responsible for your performance, regardless of what you get on the other side.

Famous acting coach, Sanford Meisner, a disciple of Stanislavski, developed a technique, based on honest emotional reactions. This training is very effective and many actors boast (rightfully) that they are Meisner trained. This technique can go wrong in the audition room, however. I believe that this is because the spontaneous repetition exercises that Meisner employs, assume that the other actor in the scene will provide emotion or energy. You might end up reading with a corpse or a robot, which could stimulate a reaction but maybe not the one appropriate for the scene. Therefore the actor must be prepared to draw upon his own inspiration.

Can I physically interact with the casting director?

Don't expect a casting director or the reader to give you physical interaction. (It could happen but let it be on their terms, not yours.) Find your own motivation. During *Solomon Kane* castings, one actor was auditioning for the role of a prisoner who was being roughed up by Kane. I read the line with her and after an uninspired reading she said, 'I expected more physical contact from you'. Don't expect anything from us. It's your job to create the circumstances, not ours. This may well be the case on set as well.

Can I expect to do more than one take?

You may only get one take, so this is why it's crucial to enter prepared and warmed up. If you are only offered one take, feel free to ask for another one. They might say no, but they won't knock you sideways for asking. When you do the second take, ask if they want you to try something different. I recommend that you come prepared with at least two choices in case you do get another chance. Then the director will see your range. They may possibly be testing to see how consistent you are too, so that's why it's good to ask. The caster may ask you to do it again, and give you some direction or she may ask you to play with it.

What if I'm wrong for the role, should I audition anyway?

Yes, absolutely. It's a meeting with a casting director. If you're not right for this role, she'll remember you for another one. Whatever you do, don't decide that you're wrong for the role before you get to your meeting: let us do that. If you believe you're wrong for the role, then you've already lost it. If you were invited, then obviously someone thinks you're right for it. Stay open and realize that they might want to cast against type.

Priscilla John explains: 'Ed Stoppard came in to meet the director Julian Jarrold for the role of Bridley on *Brideshead Revisited*. He said, "I'm not right for this." I said "That's my job down the drain, thanks very much. Just read the role and get on with it." And he got the role and he was brilliant.'

Dustin Hoffman didn't want to play Benjamin Braddock in *The Graduate* because he insisted that he wasn't right. He called it 'the biggest miscasting mistake anyone could make . . . this is a mark of a great director'.[3]

What if the character is totally alien to me?

Find a way to connect with the character. What does the character want that is like what you want? Actor Robert Carlyle is one of the most pleasant actors I've worked with. He played Hitler in CBS's *Hitler: The Rise of Evil.* His off screen personality is about as similar to Adolf Hitler as Godzilla is to Bugs Bunny. How did he pull off the role of one of history's most horrific villains? He found a way to connect with the role. 'Hitler lost his mother when he was very young, just as I did,' said Carlyle. He didn't play Hitler like a monster. Hitler didn't think he was a monster after all.

I get so nervous. What can I do?

'If you're nervous it means you care,' said Sarah Jessica Parker.[4] Nerves are your allies. Nerves give us energy, enthusiasm and excitement. Turn the energy towards the role. Even when actors say they're nervous, it doesn't always show, so don't announce it to the auditioners.

> If you're not nervous, you won't be very good. But when you come in, hang the nerves on the hook. You can collect them on the way out. When you're in the room, don't be nervous.
>
> Ros Hubbard, Casting Director

What advice can you give ethnic actors?

I realize that actors from various ethnic backgrounds feel at a disadvantage when it comes to casting in the UK and US. The truth is that there is a lot of work for

---

[3] Inside the Actors Studio, James Lipton, Bravo TV.
[4] Ibid.

ethnic actors. Firstly, casting has opened up tremendously from the old studio times. In the early days of film, actors worked only if they had a contract with a studio, and it was a certain type of actor who was invited to join the club. Films from the forties feature white icons, with perfect figures and teeth. In the fifties and early sixties, actors like Cary Grant and Doris Day, could make it; white actors, painted by the make-up department, played ethnic roles.

In the sixties and seventies we saw the emergence of leading men like Dustin Hoffman (who at one time would only have played character roles). Influenced by the auteurs of Europe, American directors started to people their films with actors who looked like real people; actors like Al Pacino and Barbra Streisand don't seem very alternative to us now, in a time when Denzel Washington and Lucy Liu can be stars. Francis Ford Coppola collaborating with legendary casting director, Fred Roos, was one of the first American directors to cast non-actors because they looked right for the part. Coppola claims, 'I was not looking for stars. I was looking for people who would be believable to me as real Italian-Americans. . .'[5] He also assiduously chose his extras, lending *The Godfather* that realistic, earthy look. He had to fight tooth and nail with the studio to cast Pacino. The studio executives were suggesting names like Robert Redford, Warren Beatty, and Ryan O'Neal to play Michael Corleone. Coppola claims that 'they told me Al was too scruffy and looked too much like a gutter rat to play a college boy'.

The trend has continued. Now when I'm casting a film that takes place in modern-day New York or London, the production insists that I cast actors of all colors of the rainbow, to reflect the real demographics of these cities. Being an ethnic actor can very often work for you, so don't let it limit you. Producer Fred Roos (who cast *The Godfather*) comments, 'The more talented and perceptive casting directors, and directors are eager to reflect what the population is in the US. In my city, half the businesses I visit, the person running the business or minding the counter, speaks with an accent, Indians, Latinos, etc. If you're casting with a brain, you should reflect that'.

At a casting symposium in the UK one actor, who was originally from an Arab country, asked how he could prevent being typecast. John Hubbard answered:

[5] Biskind, Peter. *Easy Riders, Raging Bulls: How the Sex 'n' Drugs 'n' Rock 'n' Roll Generation Saved Hollywood*. Bloomsbury, 1998.

'Well, one thing about being typecast is that you're working. I know that it's a particular problem with Arab actors in London and they all the time get the terrorist roles and the suicide bomber roles, but when you talk to them at least they're working non-stop. Now, if you want to change the kind of roles you want to go out for — there is a pigeon holing unfortunately and you can say a lot of casting directors are responsible for that — but in my opinion actors are brilliant at playing themselves. Very few actors are Daniel Day-Lewis. Thousands of actors have comfortable careers playing themselves . . .'

Casting director Maureen Duff added: 'I cast a British TV two part series called *Burn Up* . . . and there's a part of a computer scientist who gets lost in the Saudi desert and goes on the run. First the director wanted the actor to look Asian, then he changed to Irish, same part, and I had to keep bringing in different people and for whatever reason, we went around four different ways that this could be played. This was coming from BBC Executives. We ended up with a guy named San Shella but he was the very first person I called in for that part. He was having a bad day on that first audition day . . . We saw everyone and I was at my wits end, but I knew that San Shella was the one for the part so I brought him in again, put him on tape secretly, and he got the part and he's brilliant; I think his background is half Indian and half African. You wouldn't typecast him in anything.'

Is it harder for women to get cast?

There are more roles for men than women, especially in film. This is primarily because men run the industry. Men are still producing, writing and directing the majority of projects. On top of that America's film industry markets towards the 12–22 year-old boy demographic. No wonder women don't go to films as often — we're not interested in these wet dream fantasias.

It is within women's reach to change this. Women need to start writing, creating, producing, directing their own work. Join Women in Film and TV (WFTV) or similar organizations that encourage and support women. If you're not a gorgeous stick insect and you want to be an actor, then create a project about a character who is a little overweight, with a crooked nose and a space between her front teeth (or however it is you look) for yourself. When the product is good, there will be an audience. Female actors need to join the ranks with the males who have made it.

I am giving unconventional advice in an industry where producers and casters discuss an actor's 'f***ability' as if it's a real thing. Some casting directors will tell you that looks are important and that only the beautiful female actors will make it. I believe that it is fully within our power to change this. At a casting panel Ros Hubbard commented on how critical women are of one another and that we need to start supporting each other.

How can I find out about castings?

In a perfect world, your agent will do this for you but we don't live in a perfect world. It is your job to find the work for yourself. Casting director Beatrice Kruger says, 'You have to make sure that you're visible. If you have an agent, fine, but you can do the same thing if you don't have an agent. You have to take your life in your hands'. Stay on top of what's going on. There is no one door to knock on or one number to call with all of the possibilities neatly listed for you. It's about keeping your ear to the ground, reading the trade magazines like *PCR (Production and Casting Reports)* in the UK; *Variety*, *The Hollywood Reporter*, and *Screen International*. Online there are numerous websites such as IMDBpro.com that list studio and independent projects in pre-production. It is absolutely essential to make the investment and register with the major databases that casting directors use. They are Spotlight in the UK, E-talenta in Europe, Breakdown Services in the US, and Showcast and IACD in Australia.

When you put yourself up for a project, make sure that you know the breakdown and that there is a role appropriate for you. Casting directors are project oriented, not actor oriented. When I was absolutely obsessed with finding African centaurs for *Prince Caspian*, I ignored submissions from Swedish female actors that land on my desk.

When film isn't happening, turn to the theatre. Actor Graham McTavish advises, 'Ring theatres to find out what is being cast. They will, on the whole, be happy to tell you (apart from the few whose "policy" it is not to talk to actors, and they do exist). When you know what is being cast, do your homework and submit yourself for the specific role that is right for you. Don't pester, be polite and patient, but don't be afraid. Remember the only reason theatres exist is because of the actors who perform the plays. You can take every single element of a modern theatre away, even the writers, and actors would still be able to create theatre. Without them, it ceases to exist'.

If I want a film career, will I ruin it by doing commercials?

But don't knock commercials for yourself. You learn a lot . . . how to work fast, hit your mark and learn your lines.

John Hubbard, Casting Director, London

I once paneled a casting symposium and asked the panelists to give advice to young actors at the start of their careers. One casting director told them to do commercials, and a director said not to. Once again it's not simple and there are no rules. From a financial point of view alone, it is absurd to turn down an opportunity that could possibly pay your entire college debt, not to mention the fact that a commercial will get you exposure. Actors have even signed with top agents and managers as a result of commercial work.

There is a risk that you could get too much exposure on a particular ad that will make casters unable to see you in a serious role. If you are doing commercials, make sure that you keep your 'commercial package' separate from your 'film acting package'.

Actors who send composites of several photos on one page (like at a modeling agency) rather than a headshot will not be taken seriously for a film role. Actors who groom themselves to nurture a more 'commercial' look, might be too 'modelly' looking to play a 'real person' for film.

This is where good management is instrumental. Manager Lainie Sorkin of Management 360 in LA nurtured actor Orlando Jones's career by booking a 7-Up commercial spot for him in which he created and played a fun character. This move succeeded in bringing in more interesting film work for him.

Questions to ask about commercials

What is the product? Do you want to be identified as the toilet bowl man for many years to come?

Who are the creatives? Michael Bay, Spike Jones, and Oliver Stone all direct commercials. Landing a commercial with one of them or even being seen by them in a callback could start a valuable relationship.

How long does the commercial air and in what medias? TV? Print? Radio?

Where does the commercial air? If you're an American actor, maybe it's OK to be the toilet bowl man in Japan, for example.

How much is the buy-out, in what countries, and for how long?

Keep track of when and how often the ad appears. I have heard too many horror stories about productions and even agents who pocketed the money when an ad re-appeared beyond the terms of the buy-out.

When auditioning for a commercial most of the same rules apply as for film or TV casting. Make specific choices, know your type, be yourself and keep open to play. Improvisation is a particularly useful skill in commercial auditions. The difference between a commercial and a film casting is that the ultimate goal is to sell a product. Know the product that you're selling and the specific ad campaign.

Commercial casting director Maya Kvetny suggests:

* Find out something about the character and then dress to fit the part

* Be self-confident and at ease, never arrogant

* Smile naturally

* During your introduction, which in a commercial casting may be the only speech the director will hear, say something interesting and real but not drawn out

* Connect calmly to the casting director and listen to what the action is

* Ask pertinent questions. Is this a comedy or dramatic spot? Should I play it campy or natural? Most actors never ask any questions in a casting, and it can make a big difference in your performance.

What if I can't do what the director asks or I get poor direction at an audition?

George Lucas was known to scream, 'OK. Same thing only better'[6] while directing *Star Wars*. I believe that actors very often get poor direction in castings, either

---

[6] Biskind, Peter. *Easy Riders, Raging Bulls: How the Sex 'n' Drugs 'n' Rock 'n' Roll Generation Saved Hollywood*. Bloomsbury, 1998.

from the casting director or the director himself. Casting directors come from a variety of backgrounds, not all of them actor oriented. Successful directors might come from editing, writing, or even stunts or special effects, so the chances are very good that they don't understand actors. Translate their directions into actor language. Find a playable action, even if you're not given one. If a director gives you a strange direction like, 'I want her funkier', then figure out how you can turn that into an action. A student in my class was once acting a scene in which he was trying (too hard) to play a crazy guy. He was playing an adjective (crazy) rather than an action. I told him to imagine that there were snakes coming out of the other actor's head. Once he did that, and made the image real for himself, we all believed that he was crazy. Give yourself a direction that is something you can play.

Some directors give good playable directions. I observed Duane Clark in a callback for the TV series, *The Philanthropist*. We were casting a guest star character named Bejan who was described as an extremely dangerous mafia leader. A less astute director might have told the actors to play him more dangerously. Well how do you play 'dangerous?' Duane instructed the actors to 'intensely study the other character'. This was something actors could instantly play and it produced the desired effect. If the director isn't clever enough to give playable actions, you have to think for him.

How can I find out what the director wants before the casting?

You can't know for sure, and sometimes it's hopeless because they don't even know what they want until they see it. When actors read at the auditions, it is often the first time the director hears the words of the script coming to life. It's a learning curve for them. 'The character forms in the casting,' says director John Strickland. 'It's the role made flesh.' Concentrate on what you can bring and your choices. Research the project so you arrive with an informed point of view.

Can I get cast from a show reel?

Yes, I have seen actors get cast only from show reels, so it's advantageous to have a good one. Other times, the director isn't interested in looking at reels and only wants to meet actors. Generally, it's an excellent screening device if the actor is far away or if we only know his work from stage.

What if I'm bombing my casting?

Ethan Hawke noted that, 'the beauty of film acting is cultivating accidents and spontaneity'.[7] Mistakes and accidents offer opportunities for actors. One of the most memorable scenes in film history was in *Midnight Cowboy* when Dustin Hoffman's character almost walks into a taxi and yells at the taxi driver, 'I'm walking here!' This was an accident. The taxi driver was not supposed to cross through set at that time. If the casting director's phone rings during the casting, try playing it in the scene or use the frustration you feel when you go up on a line to invest it into the character.

What can I do to push the job through after the meeting?

You can send a post card with your headshot on it to the casting director, thanking him for considering you. Then you've reminded him of your interest in a professional way. Maybe if it's a choice between you and one other actor and they're undecided; your courtesy may make the difference. Generally however, there's not a thing you can do once you've left the room.

Actors seem to delight in making themselves crazy. 'On that third take we did and you asked me to internalize the second speech more, did I do it? I think I understand now what you were asking. Can I try again?' This was a text message I received from an actor over the weekend after a casting. Don't obsess. After the casting is over, forget about it. There's nothing more you can do about it.

I've met actors who arrive saying, 'I'm so embarrassed about last time. I'm so sorry'. I don't have the slightest idea what they're talking about. That means either they didn't do so badly or that it has simply disappeared from my mind as it wasn't so important for me. For casters it is usually only good or odd performances that really stand out over time.

[7] Inside the Actor's Studio, James Lipton, Bravo TV.

Obsessing over the role after the casting won't affect the outcome and you will only tie yourself into knots. Try not to invest too much hope, emotion or importance to each casting. Remember that there will always be more. If your entire well being, either emotional or financial, is caught up with one particular job, that desperation will come through in your audition and it is likely to ruin your chances.

How can I get feedback after a casting?

You can't. Don't expect it. I would suggest that you don't ask for it. It puts the casting director on the spot and you might not like the answer. The truth can sometimes be unhelpful and hurtful. Often, I can't even give feedback because the director won't share his thoughts. Actors don't get cast for silly reasons and knowing the reason might be counter-productive for you. It matters little what one director thinks of you. Gene Hackman was nominated least likely to succeed before he was kicked out of acting school. I'm glad he didn't listen to the opinion of the school's director. Allow yourself to harbor the thought that you were brilliant but the role just wasn't right for you, and move on.

When can I expect to be contacted about a role after the casting?

This varies widely. On some projects, I'm meeting actors months before shooting begins. TV projects on the other hand, often turn over very quickly. Sometimes no news is bad news and other times no news is no news. I've put an actor on tape in October for a role that shoots in March, and I get the approval to cast them three days before shooting. Stay in touch with the production, via your agent, about conflict dates etc (for example, if you get hired on another job which will disqualify you) and otherwise go on with your life.

Should I sleep with the casting director?

You can but it won't matter. Even if the casting director loves you, she is not ultimately the one who decides who plays the role. It's usually several people who make up the team which decides so by the time you've figured out who they are, and slept with all them, they've probably already cast the role.

13

FAQs about casting directors, agents and managers

What's the difference between an agent and a casting director?

An agent works for the actor and the casting director works for production. It's the difference between buying (casting director) and selling (agent). These people should be separate. If your agent is also the casting director then he is a servant of two masters, and you might lose out since the production is the more powerful master. In smaller cities it can happen that an agent will cast a film. In larger cities where the industry is more developed this practice is not considered professional. The Casting Directors' Guild of Great Britain, Casting Society of America and the International Network of Casting Directors bar casting directors who are agents or managers.

How can I make contact with a casting director?

Although the 'correct' way for an actor to be introduced is via an agent, it is not unusual for actors to send material directly to casting directors. How do you know it won't be thrown in the bin? You don't, but one way to help to prevent that is by enclosing a self-addressed, stamped envelope (SASE). Never ask for material to be returned to you without an SASE.

When is a good time to call a casting director? Never. I would suggest never calling. There's too great a chance that you'll catch them in the middle of a stressful project. Writing gives the recipient time to consider. Cover your bases by both emailing and posting hard copies. Be efficient and effective when communicating with casting directors. Ask yourself who you are contacting and why. Don't write a long sprawling cover letter; it won't be read. Write a concise letter getting right to point of why you're appropriate for their casting pool. For example,

Dear Nancy Bishop,
I see that you're casting *Karate Story 3*. I'm an experienced actor, with a black belt in karate. I also speak passable Chinese. Please find my photo and CV.
    Thanks for your consideration.
    Len Chu

If I'm looking specifically for karate guys, this actor will be called in. Research the project before you blindly send out your material. Think about your resources and costs. Hone in on the specific casting directors who are casting projects for which you are appropriate, rather than just sending your details out to every caster that you can find. Casting directors are seeking specific actors for specific roles.

Priscilla John discusses casting *Mama Mia*: 'A lot of dancers and singers wrote to me and a lot of them didn't have agents . . . Rachel Dunn sent her photo and CV. She also rang, and asked my assistant if we've got her photo, and I was passing by the desk, and I said, "Call her in." She and Ashley Lily had never done any TV, never been in front of a camera, and they're both playing major supporting roles. It does work [to submit yourself for a casting], because they knew what we were looking for — actors who could sing and dance — and it was very specific. What I can't stand is somebody saying, "I want to play that lead role", when they're clearly not ready for it.'

Most casting directors do not want actors to stop by their office personally, for the same reason that they don't like to be phoned. They're tied-up with a particular project and don't have time to sit and have cups of tea with random actors. They prefer to meet actors as part of the casting process. Casting directors will occasionally have a general meeting, with a new actor in town, but this would be arranged through agents or managers.

An actor complained during a casting symposium that she felt like a 'file corpse' on dusty shelves in casting offices, but London caster Emma Style came through with an example of just how indirectly the casting process can work. She described working with Franco Zeffirelli: 'We did *Tea with Mussolini* six or eight years ago now. [But recently] He phoned me up and he asked me about "that boy we met in the hotel". And I thought, "Oookaaay!" And he was right. We met two boys in a hotel. I'd forgotten. Luckily I had the lists and I could find them. He didn't remember the name but he did remember the essence of the boy. The reason I could find the boy he was talking about is because I had the list, and I could recognize the wallpaper on the tape behind him.' So six years after an actual casting, Zeffirelli considered the actor in another film.

It's true that your photo and CV might sit on a shelf for a long time. That doesn't mean that you have no chance. Casting director Anja Dihrberg reminds actors 'to send or email your material, with updates — what you're doing in the theatre or TV for example — so that we are still informed about your career and sometimes I can meet someone three or four years in advance [of casting them] because there are so many actors who we can't cast at the particular moment. We will remember you when the right time comes'. Regardless of how you contact us make sure that you are available and visible at all times. That means having an internet presence; see Part 3.

How do I find an agent?

Work and be visible. Make your own projects when you're not getting offers. Do showcases and take classes. If you're doing good theatre work or training in a quality course, you will attract the attention of an agent. Simply sending your photo and resume to every agency you can find is not the way. Good agencies get hundreds of these blind solicitations every day. An actor once asked me how he could make an agent watch his show reel? You can't guarantee that your material will even be opened so you have to target specific agents with specific requests. Invite agents to a project and attach reviews of your work. Instead of sending thousands of pictures in a huge envelope, send a post card with one image and a succinct message with a website address on the back. Keep cards with photos in your wallet in case you run into a good contact during the course of your day.

Research the agencies that are available to you and identify a good match. Everyone wants to be represented by the A-list agencies, but if you're at the start of your career you may have to work your way up. Research also means networking, which includes asking actors, teachers, casting directors and other industry professionals to recommend agents. IMDB provides a list of agencies, including their star-meter rankings; the lower the agency ranking, the more star names they represent. In the US, Breakdown Services and the *Ross Reports* list agencies. In the UK, look at *The Actor's Yearbook* or Spotlight's *Contacts*. Gauge each agency's clientele and whether or not you fit. In addition to considering the calibre of actor they represent, examine what types sit on their roster. Would you complement or compete with their other clients? Some agencies specialize in particular types; the Willow agency in London represents small people, for example. In most cases, you'll be looking for a local agent. Unless you're a star, it is unlikely that a London, New York or LA based agent will accept an actor living elsewhere.

Take the trouble to learn the agency's submission policies. Some agencies categorically reject submission without an industry referral. That means you need a recommendation from someone they trust. Ask a director or producer you've worked with if you can use their name when contacting an agent. Personal contacts or friends registered in the same agency could help too.

Watch out for scams. It is normal and expected that agents will take a percentage of your salary. This is how they make their living. In most cases, the percentage should be no more than ten percent. If it's a SAG (Screen Actors Guild) contract, this fee is often taken off the top of your salary (i.e. production adds ten percent for the agent). If it is a non-SAG contract, expect them to take a bite out of your wages. Check this before you sign on the dotted line.

Any reputable British or North American agent will not charge you a fee to accept you. I have heard reports of so called 'agents' who charge a fee for administration, photos and website entry, or insist that clients attend expensive in-house training. These are not agents but scam artists.* Their job is to promote you, find you work, and *then* take a commission — not before. Talk to other registered actors before you sign. To investigate the legitimacy of a US agency, check the ATA (Association of Talent Agents) website to see if they're registered. Agents with SAG and Equity associations are also held to professional standards.

> *It's the agent's job to get actors considered ... then it's up to the actor to win it.*
>
> Jeremy Conway, Conway, VanGelder, Grant, London

---

* There are extras agencies which traditionally charge a registration fee, but you should not expect the personalized treatment that you will get at a proper actor's agency.

Above all remember that even once you've signed with an agent, self-promotion and networking continues. Don't expect an agent to solve all of your problems. An agent can get you a more effective contract, more money, a better dressing room etc, but they can't get the work for you. Casting director Bonnie Gillespie discusses actors who are desperate to sign with agents, believing that they will suddenly become enormously successful working actors. She says, 'After actors sign', I often begin hearing ... "He doesn't do anything for me." "I never go out on auditions." ... Before you had an agent, all you needed in the world ... was an agent. Okay. Once you had an agent, the only reason you're not a working actor is because your agent isn't working hard enough for you. ... It does you no good to think that getting an agent will get you more auditions, and it does you no good to blame your agent for the fact that you're not getting more auditions. Some people hustle. The same people who hustled before they got an agent tend to continue to hustle after they sign agency contracts.'[1]

What is the difference between an agent and a manager? Do I need both?

> A personal manager advises and counsels talent and personalities in the entertainment industry. Personal managers have the expertise to find and develop new talent and create opportunities for those artists which they represent. Personal managers act as liaison between their clients and the public and the theatrical agents, publicists, attorneys, business managers, and other entertainment industry professionals who provide services to the personal manager's clients.
>
> The National Conference of Personal Managers' website

Managers are more common in the US than in the UK and Europe. In Los Angeles and New York many actors have both an agent and a manager because actors need all the support they can get in such competitive markets.

[1] Gillespie, Bonnie. *Self-Management for Actors: Getting Down to (Show) Business.* Cricket Feet Publishing. Los Angeles, 2009.

The agent actively procures work for an actor, while the manager is meant to work cooperatively with the agent to manage the process. Legally speaking, managers are not allowed to find work for their clients, though almost all of them do. Managers take on actors who they believe in, and view their relationship as a long term collaboration. Managers typically sign three year contracts while for agents a one year contract is common. The great advantage is that managers concentrate on a smaller number of clients than an agent. While agencies might promote packages of actors, a manager takes time to promote you as an individual artist.

> *We as a breed have an overview. That's one of the key things that differentiates us from agents. Agents by definition have larger lists of people they work with. On a daily basis I work with eight or ten people. A good manager is a very handy person to have on your side.*
>
> Derek Power, Manager

Tammy Rosen, a manager at Affirmative Talent Management notes that, 'A large agency may have a five minute phone call to promote ten actors, but a manger will use that same five minutes to promote one actor'.

In exchange for their focused attention, managers may in turn extract a higher commission than an agent, taking as much as fifteen to twenty percent of your salary. This would be in addition to your agency's fee. Clarify this with a manager from the start. The TMA (Talent Mangers Association) and the NCOPM (National Conference of Personal Managers) ensure that managers maintain professional and ethical practices.

Brad Pitt has a manager but so does Wendy Wannarole, who is at the beginning of her career. How a manager works with a star is different from how she will work with a less matured talent. Rosen uses the metaphor of a company to describe how the manager works with someone like Brad Pitt: 'The way I see it, the actor is the owner of the company and the manager is the president of the board of directors. The board is composed of the agent, the publicist, the make-up artist, and the lawyer etc'. The manager manages this team. Ideally the manager is in a position to nurture the actor, specifically guiding not only his career choices, but also his image and his relationships with specific producers, casting directors, and industry professionals. The manager could go out on a limb specifically spinning the client for a particular role.

In the case of Wendy Wannarole, the manager may be the one who actually positions her with a prestigious agency. 'An agent might say to a manager, for example, "Let me know when she's viable. Show me something that will make her more interesting than the other clients in my agency",' explains Rosen. Less well-known actors get lost in larger agencies, which is why a manager is pivotal. The manager is also more likely to handle a complicated transaction, like getting a foreign actor an O-1 Visa for example. Many European actors land a manager before an agent for that reason.

Associates and assistants

Learn the names of the people who answer the phones and monitor the reception rooms. They could be your greatest allies. Our assistants report to us about actors who were rude and pushy in the waiting room. We also respect our assistants' opinions and yes, they can make suggestions about whom we see. It goes without saying that actors, like all people on the planet, should be kind and courteous to everyone, but especially to assistants, who may become associates and eventually casting directors themselves.

Part 3

Marketing: the tools of the trade

> *To be crude you are a product and you have to market yourself to get attention on the market place.*
>
> John Hubbard, Casting Director, London

Good actors need to be good business people. Marketing is a nauseating idea to many actors who just want to be artists, but this profession is not for the faint hearted. Is it your agent's job to market you? Yes, but you need to take responsibility for your own career. That means researching productions and job opportunities. Part 3 is about the essential tools that all actors need to create a marketing strategy:

* Branding

* Headshot

* Resume

* Show reel

* Video resources

* Online presence

Pippa Harrison, who works for the leading UK casting service, Spotlight, advises actors to 'get in the habit, half an hour everyday, of doing research. Know what theatres are re-casting and when. Do that all the time so that you become part of the industry that you're working in'.

14 Archetypes for actor branding

When I trained at the National Theatre Institute, I performed a monologue for casting directors, who visited the school. I chose Pheobe's speech about being rejected by Orlando in *As You Like It* because I thought it was funny. The casting director looked at me and said, 'But you're Rosalind, not Phoebe'. She was right — I didn't get it. I couldn't play the dumb, comic country girl. I had to play the city slicker. In *Little Miss Sunshine*, Olive Hoover wanted so much to be a beauty queen, but she couldn't see that she wasn't like the pornographically pretty girls around her at the competition. There was no doubt, however, that she was the most extraordinary girl there. Know your archetype.

Actors want to play all roles, and perhaps they can at some point in their careers. But if you want to be employable, remember that casting directors, producers and writers think in terms of characters and types. In psychology and mythology it's called archetype; in marketing it's called branding. The more competitive the market, the more an actor has to brand himself, to make himself special, and unique in his product niche.

While on the one hand I would say that some of the most brilliant casting choices have deliberately gone against type, there is nothing wrong with typecasting. Remember the second part of the word typecast is cast. Actors often resist the idea of types because it reminds them of stereotypes: a derogatory over-simplification of character. Archetypes, however, have existed in show business for centuries, starting with the masked Greek dramas, to Commedia dell'Arte, to Shakespeare, to the sit-coms of today. An archetype refers to the original model of a person or, in the words of psychologist Karl Jung a 'symbolic figure' or a 'collective representation' of a person, drawn from 'the universal symbolism' that we share. Audiences connect with archetypes.

Vin Diesel, who is racially and ethnically nebulous, made a film about his frustration with typecasting. He produced, directed and acted in *Multi-Facial* early in his career, or rather before he *had* a career. It was about an actor who continually fell between the cracks at castings for Italian-Americans, Hispanics, or African Americans. He never got the job. In the process, Diesel branded himself, created his own character and type, which ironically has made him famous. The lesson is to know thyself and what you can play well. If no one is casting you, cast yourself and show us how to cast you. Once you start getting work, you can branch out, and develop work in other archetypes.

Here are examples of epic archetypes from films we know:
The Innocent - Dorothy in *The Wizard of Oz*
Orphan — Oliver Twist
Warrior — Aragon in *Lord of the Rings*
Caregiver — Hanna the Nurse in *The English Patient*
Creator — Aslan in *Narnia*
Seeker — Harry Potter
Lover — Will Turner in *Pirates of the Caribbean*
Destroyer — The Wicked Witch in *The Wizard of Oz*

Ruler — Queen Elizabeth I in *Elizabeth*
Magician — Gandalf in *Lord of the Rings*
Sage — Ben Obi Wan Kenobi in *Star Wars*
Fool — Donkey in *Shrek*

Here are more general archetypes listed with famous actors who play them.

Family archetypes

The father — Liam Neeson in *Love Actually*
The mother — Brenda Blethyn in *Atonement*

Story archetypes

The hero — Gerard Butler in *300*
The maiden — Scarlett Johansson in *The Girl with the Pearl Earring*
The wise old man — Morgan Freeman in *The Shawshank Redemption*
The witch or sorceress — Tilda Swinton in *Narnia*
The trickster — Jack Nicholson in *The Witches of Eastwick*

Archetypes have morphed to include these more specific types that appear in today's film, TV and commercial projects:

Male	Female
Computer geek	Bimbo
Footballer	Football wife
Bouncer	Cheerleader
Rapper	Feminist
Hustler	Bag lady
Mob boss	Mafia wife
The stag night bloke	The trafficked sex worker

Male or female	Children
Doctor	Precocious child
Lawyer	Abused child
CEO	Skateboarder
Night clubber	Nerd
Junkie	Fat kid
Couch potato	Popular kid

It's useful for actors to identify their archetypes (also called primary types, casting brackets or niches). When you put your product on the marketplace, customers want to know what they're buying. You'll use your archetypes as part of your branding process. Knowing your archetypes helps you select an image for a headshot. A headshot is a neutral photo of an actor's face and is often the first thing a casting director sees. Choosing a primary archetype doesn't mean that you have to stick with this one type only. Look at Tilda Swinton. I have listed her as the witch archetype because of her role in *Narnia*, but she just as deftly played the CEO in *Michael Clayton*. Archetypes will morph and change during an actor's lifetime. Judi Dench has made the jump from playing the lover, Juliet, when she was young, to the dowdy old Queen Elizabeth in recent years. You can shoot a variety of headshots that are within your range and present specific ones for different roles.

Casting director Bonnie Gillespie suggests 'watching TV, commercials, films and plays with a notepad ... to see what types are out there to be able to determine what primary type you are'. Look at your CV and see if there is a trend. Are you playing mostly the naughty girl, the prostitute, the mother, or the nurse? Think about working actors who are playing the roles that you want to play and investigate how these actors present themselves. If you struggle to fit in, then follow in the footsteps of performers like Vin Diesel who created his own archetype.

Knowing your archetype is part of knowing yourself — as a person and as an artist. I once taught a very good American actor who had a lovely warm quality and easily fit in the range of lover, father, teacher, businessman, etc. When I was casting a Russian mafia hit-man role he wrote and asked if he could audition for it. I was fairly shocked that he didn't know himself well enough to know that role was well out of his range. Conversely, don't limit yourself too much. Face the challenge to push past the archetypes within your comfort zones. I once assigned an actor an aristocratic character and he said, 'I only play lower class roles'. He gave up a great chance to stretch himself. In Chapter 11, I discuss examples of actors who come to an audition believing they can't play a role, even when the casting director has invited them. Challenge yourself to grow, and allow your archetypes to shift as you advance through your career.

Things to remember from this chapter

* Know thyself

* Identify the archetypes you want to play and can play well

* Knowing your archetype will help you to create one central image for your marketing campaign

* Typecasting is not necessarily negative; if you're typecast, it means you're working

* Don't limit your range; work to push past your archetypes as well

Headshots

> *All photos are accurate. None of them is the truth.*
>
> Richard Avedon, Photographer

A good headshot is an accurate photo, spun to get you the most work possible. That does not mean spinning the photo so that you look a thousand times better than in life. The biggest mistake that actors make is presenting themselves inaccurately. Namely their headshots don't look like them. Casting directors want the person who walks into the room to look exactly like their headshot. That means a current shot, with your hair, eyebrows, beard, teeth, reasonably the same as it will be on the day of the casting.

Guidelines for headshots

Bonnie Gillespie reminds us that a 'headshot isn't a photo. It's a marketing tool'. Use it to 'show us how to cast you'.[1] A successful headshot will:

Look exactly like you. This can't be emphasized enough. One hundred percent of casting directors at CSA agreed that the most important aspect of the headshot is that it looks like the actor. Everyone wants to look like their best self, so you're not going to portray yourself as you would be getting out of bed on New Year's morning. Headshot photographer Natasha Merchant says, 'A good headshot captures the person looking exactly as they would if you caught them walking down the street on a very good day'.

[1] Gillespie, Bonnie. *Self-Management for Actors: Getting Down to (Show) Business.* Cricket Feet Publishing. Los Angeles, 2009.

Figure 15.1 The expression is a perfect blend of neutral yet interesting. The slight smile really works for this actress as it softens a strong face and it also draws us into the image. Photo of Christine Adams by Natasha Merchant

> *When I want to photograph someone, what it really means is that I'd like to know them. Anyone I know I photograph.*
>
> Annie Leibovitz, Photographer

Reveal the actor's personality. We should *know* you in your photo. I've emphasized that the actor's unique style, presence, personality, chemistry is what interests casting directors the most. One recalls the scene in *Zooland* where Ben Stiller playing a model, demonstrates his silly poses, like 'blue steel', for photo shoots. This is a great example of what *not* to do for a headshot session. You want to look as natural and relaxed as possible so that inimitable thing that makes you *you* is revealed. The idea that certain aboriginal people won't allow their photo to be taken for fear of losing their soul, may have some relevance in that a good picture will capture the essence and humanity of that person.

Feature active, thinking eyes. While I advise *against* looking directly into camera at a casting, shooting a headshot is the opposite story. The eyes should look directly into the lens. Just as film acting is based on expressing and communicating through the eyes, a headshot should reflect a thought process. The eyes should express intention without pulling a face. Many headshot photographers use the technique of focusing sharply on the eyes, while subtly softening out towards the edges of the face so that the eyes draw in the viewer.

Suggest an archetype. The best headshots are neutral but will suggest an archetype that will help casters understand how to cast you. I do an exercise in my marketing seminars in which actors post their headshot and the class suggests what archetypes best suit them. One actor got suggestions like mob boss, criminal, and CIA spy. Yet he had a warm friendly personality, often playing the father or best friend. Since he never played these hard man types, the headshot was getting him called in for the wrong roles. He learned that his shot was not accurately representing his range of archetypes, so he got it re-shot.

While I maintain that there is an exception to every rule, I would advise **against** the following:

Heavily airbrushed photos. Show us what you really look like, warts and all. We might want the warts. (A cold sore that isn't normally part of your facial landscape warrants a slight airbrush.)

Lots of tooth. While you do want to show some teeth for commercial shots, full-on toothy smiles are not generally wanted.

Hands. Keep hands out of the shots. (I hate those photos of girls with their finger in their mouth.)

Props. Keep the shot simple. Use of too many props or gimmicks clutter the image. (Trust that we'll understand that you can play an academic, without holding a stack of books, for example.)

Specific backgrounds. Keep the background as neutral and non-specific as possible. Let the viewer imagine you in different locations.

Overly stylized photos. Make sure that the photographer's style doesn't overpower the image. Remember that the headshot is a marketing tool for you, not the photographer.

Headshots without name or contact information. I know this sounds obvious, but I have too many unknown headshots floating around in my file. If you don't include your CV with your photo, at least put your website or agency contact info on the back.

Styles of headshots

When selecting your headshot, consider to what market you are presenting. There are vastly different trends in the US and UK. One UK director complained that she was getting submissions from unprofessional actors. What appeared amateur to her were headshots done in the US. In the UK the accepted standard is still black and white, often shot outside with natural light, and cropped just under the collarbone. In the US actors are using color and are experimenting with various formats. In LA you might see a landscape format, with the actor off-centre, or cropped with half her face missing. In Europe, it's less standardized and I've seen a variety of choices. Often an agency will make their own rules and standardize the presentation of their pool of actors (see figure 15.1 as an example of a UK headshot and 15.2 for an example of a US headshot).

Ninety-nine percent of CSA members prefer color photos. A color photo provides more information. In casting it's important to know if someone has red hair or blue eyes. I hope that this trend will eventually catch on in the UK. I personally prefer the portrait format since the face tends to be more prominent than in a landscape. I dislike the strange stylized cropping techniques that US photographers are using now, where the actor isn't centered or fully displayed.

Figure 15.2 Although reproduced here in black and white this headshot of actress Elaine Loh is in colour which casting directors prefer. Photograph by Bradford Rogne

It's common sense to keep the actor in full view, rather than presenting them creatively. Use your own judgment, and bear in mind that there are no absolute rights and wrongs.

Sending your headshot

Professional presentation means sending one primary image to a casting director when auditioning for a specific role. It is fine to keep a few different headshots, earmarking specific looks for different jobs. Actors may shoot separate headshots for commercials, straight drama and musical theatre. Choose the image that fits the role. Don't confuse us with too many different looks. For example, do not even think of sending a composite with fifteen different shots. If you're responding to a general call where the role is unspecified or if you're applying to an agency, then you may send more than one photo. When sending two photos, I want the second photo to provide more or different information and a full body shot will do that. I urge actors to include photos that show their full form or at least from the waist up.

Choosing and working with your photographer

I hope it goes without saying that you should hire a professional. Yes, your Uncle Jeffrey may take great photos and offer to do it for free, but the art of shooting a professionally accepted headshot is a very specific skill. Show us that you are serious about your career by making the investment. When choosing your photographer, it's not enough to go solely on the recommendation of a friend. The chemistry that your friend had may not be there between you and that same photographer. Research her photos so that you know and like her work. All photographers have their own style so make sure their style doesn't overpower the subject matter — namely you.

Schedule an interview with the photographer before the shoot to make sure that you feel relaxed and comfortable with her. If you feel ill at ease, the photos will reflect that. Bring previous headshots as a starting point to discuss what you did and didn't like about them. Discuss archetypes and how you'd like to be cast. If you've been playing lots of doctors but would like to start broadening your range, devise ways to suggest that with subtle dress choices. If you have an agent or manager, make sure he participates in the discussion. You, the photographer and the agent should be working as a team to create your branding.

At the session itself, bring several different dress choices so you can aim for a range of looks within your archetypes. A good photographer will direct the session but don't rely solely on the photographer's inspiration. It's your job to find motivations that turn the wheels in your head, keeping your eyes engaged. You are the one in front of camera, so come prepared with ideas. Keep lines in your head from the roles you have played or that you want to play. Playing active objectives and making strong choices are effective in shoot sessions just as they are in auditions.

Above all enjoy the session. If you're in pain then so are we. The more you relax and enjoy the session, the better the photos will be.

Choosing your headshot

There was a time when casting directors worked only from stacks of 8¢¢ ¥ 10¢¢ photos. The computer age has changed this as we now view pictures as thumbnails on computers and two inch cells phone screens. When I post a breakdown on Breakdown Services or Spotlight, I get thousands of suggestions and they appear on my computer screen in thumbnail size. I peruse them, choosing the more interesting and appropriate options to explore further. Sometimes when I Google an actor, all I can find is a tiny image that refuses to enlarge, so choose a photo that also works as a thumbnail.

The biggest mistake that actors make is choosing their own headshot; in those cases we nearly always end up with the most flattering image. The most beautiful shot is not necessarily the one that will get you the most work. Consult with your agent, the photographer, teachers, classmates, and actor friends, before you make a decision. People who know you can tell if the picture 'captures' you and who you are. The disadvantage is they are biased and filter you through their own particular shade of glasses.

People who don't know you have the advantage of being completely unbiased and may give you a more balanced opinion. There are actors' websites and forums where you can post your headshot and get feedback. Ask specific questions when asking for feedback. 'What types of role do you see me playing?' or 'How would you cast me?' The opinionaters are unlikely to agree, so in the end it's your call. Choose a headshot that you are proud to hand over to casters.

> *It's one thing to photograph people. It is another to make others care about them by revealing the core of their humanness.*
>
> Paul Strand, Photographer

Digital or hard copy?

Yes, it's true that in the casting business we are increasingly relying on digital images on the internet. Fewer and fewer headshot prints pass through my hands. However, the good old 8¢¢ ¥ 10¢¢ or A4 size is still necessary and in circulation.

Always have a photo with you when you arrive at castings. Yes, your agent should have sent it, but don't rely entirely on him. Agents are fallible and casting directors lose things so take responsibility for putting it in our hands. Although the digital photo is one hundred percent essential, we are not impressed with actors who come to castings with images carried on flashcards or CDs.

Things to remember from this chapter

* Your headshot is not just a photo, it's an important marketing tool

* The headshot must look like you

* When choosing a headshot, identify your archetype and your market

* Your headshot should portray you with active eyes

* Make sure your photo stands out in thumbnail size

16

CV or resume

> *Your resume is not a list, it's spin*
>
> Bonnie Gillespie, Casting Director and Author

Your resume is not simply a list of all the work you've ever done. The CV (UK) or resume (North America) is a marketing tool edited to get you work. Never lie, but spin. Display the accurate and true facts in the order that they will best present you for the roles you want to be considered for. Some actors mistakenly think that to impress casters they should list as many projects as possible. On the contrary, this is a brilliant way to bury yourself in a sea of words. Help us by selecting your best and most relevant credits.

Tip

Make sure that all of the information on your resume is very clearly presented and itemized. CVs are laid out slightly differently in the US and UK. Lucinda Syson recounts a time when a US producer sat in on her casting session in London. All heads turned when the producer asked the actor if his hobbies were shopping and f***ing. That's apparently what she thought it said on his CV. She didn't realize that *Shopping and F***ing* is the name of a play by Mark Ravenhill.

Ignore rules that say you must list work strictly in chronological order and in a uniform way each time. Feature your most prominent work first. If your best leading role was last year, then put that project at the top, and list this year's project, in which you played the supporting role, below it. It's not a lie. It's spin.

A professional resume is generally organized as follows:

* Name in bold at the top, with contact or agent contact information

* Height in appropriate measurements. (Remember that Americans aren't familiar with the metric system and don't know what a stone in weight is)

* Color of hair and eyes

* Playing range, not age

* Union status: SAG (Screen Actors Guild) or Equity etc. If you don't have membership, skip the section entirely. (Sometimes non-SAG members are preferred on independent projects)

Trim the resume to one page, itemizing selected credits neatly in three easy-to-read columns. List your best area first. For example, if you have many strong stage credits, push them to the top. Otherwise list as follows:

* **Film**. List your best projects first. If your experience is limited, include student films and unpaid video work. Apart from naming the title of the project in the first column, there is no one right way to list your credits. In North America, actors often denote their billing in the second column. That means: lead, supporting, featured, or extra. Some actors list the name of the role, but that is less informative. Some actors simply list the project, the director and the company, without mentioning what they played in it. Make your decision based on what showcases you the best.

   In the third column, list the most impressive thing about the film. For example, mention the production company if it was produced by Universal Studios. If it was an unknown production company, but a well respected director, like Gus Van Sant, then hustle his name into the column. If it was a small independent film produced by George Lucas's company, then George Lucas gets the third column place. If everything about the film was unknown, except the star, then go ahead and mention that it starred Ben Kingsley or whoever.

* **TV** comes after film or can be listed under one heading, Film and TV. If you choose to list your billing, the standard is: series regular, recurring, guest star or co-star. Your billing should be denoted in your contract, if you have any doubt.

* **Theatre**. If you're brand new on the scene, you can list school theatre. Everyone has to start somewhere. For theatre the three columns are play, role, and the name of the theatre company and/or director (whichever is better.) If you played a lead in an unknown play, feel free to write 'Gary (lead)'.

* **Commercial/Industrial**. If you have a long list of commercial credits you may want to write, 'conflicts available upon request.' That way the commercial credits don't overwhelm your CV if you're trying to develop a film career. (Conflicts mean that when you've represented one brand of soap, you can't appear in a commercial for another brand of soap in the same year.)

* **Training**. Here you can list a university degree and any training courses or teachers with whom you're studying. If you're just starting out and your strongest suit is your education, you can list it at the top if you wish. Casters like to see that your training is ongoing.

* **Special skills**. Your skills and interests can be important in the casting process but never lie. If you ride a horse, say at what level (intermediate, recreationally, professionally, etc). If you sing, that means not only that you can carry a tune but that you sing professionally. Mention your voice range (tenor, alto, etc.) Be sure that you can really do the accents you have listed. You may have to prove it at an audition. Say whether you speak a foreign language and at what level. Say whether you have a driver's licence.

In North America the resume is stapled to the back of your photo. The other option is to include a thumbnail sized headshot in the upper left corner of your CV (I prefer left corner, because the eye reads left to right) in addition to a contrasting photo on the back. It's essential that the photo and the resume stay together.

Here is a resume that I have created for a fictional actor, Wendy Wannarole, who is just out of school and hasn't worked professionally yet.

* **Contact info**. She doesn't have an agent yet, so she has listed her own contact information and her website. Avoiding the stalkers, she has not listed her personal address or number.

* **Age range**. Wendy is 22, so she has listed her playing range as 16–26. Not all actors can get away with playing a sixteen year old, but it is a

WENDY WANNAROLE

www.wendywannarole.com

info@wendywannarole.com

Height: 5¢6¢¢
Weight: 120 lbs
Color Hair: Brown
Color Eyes: Brown
Playing Range: 18–26

TRAINING

B.A. in Acting, University of Wannabe, 2006
Shakespeare Scene Study, Barbara Gains, Chicago
Susan Bateson, New York NY.
Viewpoints Training, Ann Bogart, SITI company, New York
Film Acting, Patrick Tucker
National High School Institute — Cherubs, Northwestern University

THEATRE

Romeo and Juliet	Juliet	Sam Mendes
Wait Until Dark	Suzy	University Players
Guys and Dolls	Miss Adelaide	University of Wannabe
Oklahoma!	Chorus	University of Wannabe
The Glass Menagerie	Laura	University Players

FILM

Long Road Home	Featured	Larry Gross

Special Skills: Driver's License. Singer; Soprano. Piano. Jazz dancing. Dialects: English (RP), and Irish. Languages: Sign Language.

great advantage. Casting older actors in younger roles allows productions to work around child labor laws.

* **Training**. She has placed her training at the top since she has studied with known and respected teachers. Her theatre experience is above her film experience because it's more extensive.

* **Theatre**. You'll notice that her credits are all in university theatre ... but wait! She's got a credit directed by Sam Mendes. The famous Sam Mendes? OK, it's unlikely that he was directing at the University of Wannabe, but occasionally universities and colleges do get famous directors to come in and work with students, so she has exploited this to the fullest and listed his name instead of the name of the theatre (which no one has heard of).

* **Film**. Her film experience has been on student film projects, but she has just listed them as 'independent'.

Elaine Loh (who actually exists) is a more experienced actor than Wendy Wannarole. She has chosen to organize her resume simply in two columns, avoiding the specifics of role names and billing. This is acceptable. In her second film column, she lists the director or the production company or both depending on what is most advantageous for her. For theatre, she has traditionally listed the role, and delineated when it is a lead.

For training, she specifies her current teacher and lists other training of note. Under Special skills, notice how she has specified her skills, mentioning her scuba certification level. Elaine also had some fun listing things, like solving a Rubik's cube in less than two minutes, which might not be so useful, but could be an amusing conversation starter.

O'Neill Talent Group
Ph: 818-566-7717 Fax: 818-566-7725

ELAINE LOH
SAG/AFTRA

Weight: 115 lbs
Height: 5¢ 5¢ ¢

Demo Reel available at www.elaineloh.com

TELEVISION

Curb Your Enthusiasm	Co-star	HBO — Dir: Alec Berg
The New Adventures of Old Christine	Co-star	CBS — Dir: Andy Ackerman
Chuck	Co-star	NBC — Dir: Jay Chandrasekhar
The Young and the Restless	Co-star	CBS — Dir: Andrew Lee
What About Brian	Co-star	ABC — Dir: Bethany Rooney
Passions	Co-star	NBC — Dir: Karen Wilkens

FILM *full list upon request

Little Saigon	Dir: Sean Delgado
The Three Amigas **2008 Cannes Short Film corner	Prod: Pamela Holt, Elaine Loh
Sacred Journey	Dir: Michael Criscione
Winged Creatures (scene w/Forest Whitaker)	Dir: Rowan Woods
Pizza Guy **2008 winner Buzz Award at IFF Tribeca	CrazySane Productions
Lovers and Haters	Dir: Spike Lee
Death and Life of Bobby Z (scene w/Jason Lewis)	Warner Bros/Alcon Ent., Dir: John Herzfeld
Unscripted	Dir: Allan De Leon
How to Build a Rapper	sevenTeight Productions
The Blood Oath of 3 Men and a Baby	Dir: Sandeep Parikh — *Ch.101 selection
Death Ride	Eleven Arts Ent., Dir: Junichi Suzuki
An Uzi at the Alamo	Scarred Heel Prods, Dir: Chris Sparling

THEATER *full list upon request

Schoolhouse Rock Live!***	Dina	Greenway Court Theater, Dir: Mark Savage
Jesus' Kid Brother	Destiny Pilate	I.C.T., Long Beach, Dir: Jules Aaron
The Ohmies	Poogle (lead)	Skirball Center, and touring company
Overflow	Faith (lead)	Hudson Guild, Dir: David Lee
Midsummer Showcase	Ensemble/Lead	hereandnow theater co., Dir: John Miyasaki
Little Shop of Horrors	Chiffon	Franklin Performing Arts Co, MA
Cabaret	Kit Kat Girl	Production Workshop, Brown University
Emma	Fly Girl (supporting)	Brownbrokers Mainstage, Brown University

***Variety says: 'Elaine Loh is blessed with a lovely and powerful voice, and she lights up the stage with her energetic performances . . .'

INTERNET*full list upon request

Oprah is Dead	Comedy Central (atom.com), Dir: Clint Gage
Onesie	Cartoon Network (superdeluxe.com)

TRAINING

Acting - Stan Kirsch (current), Lesly Kahn
Improv - Upright Citizens Brigade, Will McLaughlin; The Empty Stage, Kay Christianson
Cold Reading - Brian Reise
Scene Study - Michael Woolson - Master Class
Chekhov Foundation Course - Lisa Dalton - The Chekhov Connection
Voice/Speech/Dance - Boston Conservatory, Brown University

SPECIAL SKILLS

* Languages: Spanish, Mandarin, Asian accents (Chinese/Japanese)
* Athletics: scuba diver (advanced PADI certified), pool/billiards, bowling, ping pong, Tae Bo, swimming, Frisbee, water-skiing, capable at most sports, Purple Belt mixed martial arts (study with Ken Nagayama - 1st place Form)
* Dance: tap, ballet, hip hop
* Singing/Music: Soprano (training at Brown Univ., Wellesley College), professional cabaret singer, reads music, some piano
* Other: Flexible and double-jointed, whistling, great with kids and animals, card games (poker, black jack, etc.), able to solve a Rubik's cube in less than 2 minutes, Miss Rhode Island USA 2003 Top Ten Finalist, active member of the Actor's Network, Stand-Up Comedian

Things to remember from this chapter

❋ The CV or resume is not simply a list of everything you have done

❋ Itemize your projects honestly but in a way that best showcases you

17 Showreel or demo reel

In your marketing campaign, think of the headshot and resume as your print advertisement and the reel as your commercial. A showreel or demo reel could even be the first thing a director sees. Just as the resume is not a list of all your projects, the reel is not a collection of everything you've ever done. It is a carefully edited selection of your best work. Your reel should be available to casters in hard copy as a DVD, as well as being accessable at the click of a button; that means posting it on YouTube, databases, and your website.

The image you present on the reel needs to match your primary head shot, so that's a good place to start. Begin the reel with your headshot so we have no doubt whose reel we're watching. Some actors start with a montage of different shots to introduce themselves. I am not a big fan of this but if you do have a montage keep it very short. Casters are impatient to get to the juice of the reel. Just as the headshot should be current, so should the reel. You might have been great as a child actor, but showing your baby pictures will not get you cast today.

When Shakespeare said 'brevity is the soul of wit', he must have been thinking about showreels. The shorter the better. Producers and directors don't have time to watch hours of footage. If your reel is more than two or three minutes, it's almost guaranteed that it won't be watched to the end. Zachary Weintraub of Z Productions suggests that it's better to trim a reel short and to leave them wanting more. If a casting director's curiosity about the actor is completely satisfied by the reel, then he is less likely to call him in for an audition.

Many actors miss the opportunity to sell themselves with poorly produced reels. Top mistakes include reels that

* run too long and are boring

* contain too much of one project or similar material

* feature other actors more than the presented actor

* contain the right material but the editing is slow

* are over edited with snippets that are too short to get a sense that the actor can create a whole character

* contain unprofessionally recorded theatre

* have poor sound quality

* don't include contact information

Avoid these mistakes by working with a professional editor who can help you reduce your scenes and concentrate on the good stuff. As discussed in the section about choosing a photographer, interview and familiarize yourself with your editor before you begin. Take a look at reels he's cut. Make sure that his work is a commercial for the *actor*, not for the *editor*.

Since you don't know how long the viewer will stay tuned, position your best work at the beginning of the reel. The same idea applies if you share scenes with prestigious actors; showcase these clips first because a star lends immediate legitimacy. If you can carry a scene with Tom Hanks, then you can be trusted. Urge your editor to cut right to the chase in each scene. The filmmaker who produced your material is telling a story. You're not. You are advertising your brand. Cut right into the middle of the scene, the heat of the argument, or the moment of discovery, then quickly move on to your next brilliant moment. Just as a flashlight only works on the strength of its weakest battery, so does a reel; leave out scenes that are below par.

Just as variety and contrast are interesting in a performance, such is also the case with a reel. Professional editor Weintraub advises, 'Use variation in this order: long scene, short scene, fast scene, slow scene, etc. The reel should be entertaining'. The variety should extend to the types of scenes you choose.

Intersperse comedy with tragedy, action with costume drama, etc. Remember that clips that are too short can also spoil the effectiveness of your reel. I find speechless montages of actors set to music, unhelpful. I want to see at least a few scenes that are long enough to demonstrate that the actor has created a cogent character arch, with inner depth.

Avoid two-shots in which the other actor is featured much more than you. We may end up casting your co-star instead. If you have original footage, you can play around with the editing, leaving the shot hanging on you, while the other actor's voice is off camera.

Think carefully about which clips you choose. Your favorite scene may not reflect your best work. An agent or editor is a more impartial arbitrator. Consider not just how you've *been* cast, but how you *want* to be cast and spin your choices accordingly. When negotiating your deal with the editor, establish how many cuts he'll do within the agreed fee. Circulate the first cut to directors and professionals you trust for feedback before the final cut. At the end of the day, it's *you* who must be satisfied, so make sure that you feel proud to post the final product on your website.

Learning to edit and manipulate the medium is another excellent skill for you to develop as an actor. When you're auditioning for a specific part you might want to edit together a few specific clips that will sell you specifically for that role. If your editor doesn't have time or you don't have the money to pay him, take the reigns into own hands and edit it yourself. Even technophobes can learn to edit on today's programs.

If you're just starting out . . .

If you don't have a film career yet, then creating a reel can be a daunting task. How can you cleverly cut together scenes that don't exist yet? The first question to ask yourself is, 'Am I ready to make a reel?' Make sure you've had some training before you set off. Everyone has to start somewhere. If you're not experienced on screen then your first priority should be to gain experience.

Collect footage by volunteering to appear in student films at a local film school or university. You never know when you might be working with the next Martin Scorsese, and most importantly you're getting experience in front of camera. The director might even be willing to cut a reel for you in exchange for your performance. There are always independent directors seeking actors on no or low budgets. Get connected to the circuits and networking sites that link blossoming actors and directors.

Actors just starting out can also collect footage from screen acting classes. There are productions companies that specialize in producing show reels. That means that they provide a set, lighting, and sometimes coaching, to shoot professional quality scenes specifically designed for a reel. Ultimately, it is not the reel itself that is important, so much as some kind of quality taped material. One option is to invest the money that you would have used in producing a reel and collaborate with other like-minded artists to produce a short film.

Things to remember from this chapter

* The showreel should be available to casters 24/7 at the click of a button

* Showreels should be no longer than 2-3 minutes

* Editing should reflect the variety and depth of the actor's talent

* The showreel should spin the actor for the roles she wishes to play

18

How to prepare a self audition

> " *I would say that before you ever put yourself on tape, make sure you know how — because of the amount of bad quality you see, the amount of people wondering where their motivations are . . . If you put yourself on tape . . . then for God's sakes, put yourself on tape, remember it's 'action', do it, then stop. Don't do too many takes. Don't send me seventeen takes. One or two maximum.*

Ros Hubbard, Casting Director, London

As we are working in a world market, it is more and more common for actors to film their own audition and send it to a casting director. The problem is that many actors don't know how to prepare and tape an audition properly. Instances in which a self audition are appropriate would include, when an actor is working or away from where the casting session is being held, or when there is a world wide search for a role and actors are asked to send their casting to a central place. Casting directors often open the gates when looking for child actors. On *Mr. Bean's Holiday*, Nina Gold put out a world wide casting search for the little boy, for example. Actors from all over Europe and the UK sent me audition tapes and were cast in supporting roles in Queen Latifah's *Last Holiday*. I have also cast leading characters on independent films with actors who sent tapes from around the world. Actor Elaine Cassidy was cast from a self audition tape that she sent from London to LA four days before the pilot of *Harper's Island* began. If there is ever a time when you can't go to an audition but would like to be considered, convince your agent to ask for the scene so that you can tape yourself.

At the time of writing, British website the Casting Scene (www.thecastingscene.com), is at the cutting edge of self audition technology, offering actors the opportunity to audition for selected projects online using a web cam. The breakdown and sides are available on the site; Casting Notebook in North America offers a service for actors to put themselves on tape. Spotlight and Breakdown Services also offer services to put actors on tape under professional conditions in a studio. By the time this book is published, there may be several other online casting sites offering this service.

It's important to know how to prepare an effective audition. It might sound like a piece of cake, but many actors find it hard to set up the taping themselves. As a former technophobe, I can assure you there's nothing complicated about operating a basic video camera. Learn it and consider it one of the skills that an actor should know to succeed in today's film world. The disadvantage of taping yourself is that you don't have the benefit of a caster's direction. The advantage is that you can prepare the session in the comfort of your own home, and practice with multiple takes. So take a breath and relax, here are some guidelines.

Steps in self auditioning
Equipment
Every actor should have their own camera. Video cameras are affordable and useful but high end, high tech equipment is not necessary. A secondary investment might be a separate microphone, as internal microphones are often poor. You need access to a computer as well. Mac computers still seem to rule in the film world, because of their user friendly video features, but a PC serves just as well.

Preparation
Once you get hold of the scene, follow the steps already outlined in this book. First you want to answer the basic acting questions:

* Who am I?

* Where am I?

* Who am I talking to?

* What do I want?

Shooting

* Find a solid background in your home, a plain wall or curtain. Avoid shooting in front of a window, patterned wall paper, or busy bookshelves

* Aim the camera at your eye level. Don't shoot up or down on yourself

* Begin with a short simple introduction stating your name, your agent's name, and the role. Show your body in wide angle and both profiles

* If you're reading with a scene partner (could be the camera operator) place them directly at eye level next to the camera lens. If you prefer to find a focus point, rather than reading with a person, choose a spot near the camera lens, so that we can see you

* Make sure you're well lit so that we can see your eyes. Natural lighting can work well

* Prepare two takes for each scene that you read. One should be a medium shot — from the waist or mid chest up. The other should be a close up — just the face (see Figures 18.1–3). We don't need to see a lot of ceiling space above your head (see Figure 18.4)

Figure 18.1 Extreme close up

Figure 18.2 Close up

Figure 18.3 Medium shot

* Play variety and range. If you do two takes, make each take different. There is no point in sending two versions, unless there is new information the second time around

* Make sure you're listening (see Chapter 9 on listening). Remember that a large proportion of film acting is listening and not speaking.

Figure 18.4 Make yourself the centre of attention, not the wall above your head

❋ Make sure you're miked properly. If you don't have a good external mike, make sure that you are very close to the camera. Always film your scene indoors, even if it takes place outdoors. On one self casting, the actor was trying for the role of a taxi driver. He shot the scene in his car outside and we couldn't hear a word he was saying.

Sending the casting

Send your scene as a link on the web. This gives you the advantage of speed. It can get to the casting director as soon as you upload it to a site. The disadvantage is that it is a small and sometimes tinny image. Ideally, you should send it both ways, by DVD through the post, and via a web link.

To provide a web link you can upload the casting to your own website and give the director an access code. This has the advantage of directing our attention to your site. Otherwise you can use YouTube, one of the many send file services available on the web.

If [the self audition] is not good enough, don't send it. It could go against you and haunt you for the next job. Make sure you do a good take.

Frank Moiselle, Casting Director

What not to do

I'll give you the opportunity to learn from some bad examples I've seen.

Don't try to shoot a professional film

Some actors mistakenly think that they must produce a mini film and go out of their way to acquire costumes, sets, and professional editing. ('You should watch my tape for the locations alone,' one actor said to me. Indeed, that was the best part!) One tape that was sent to me for *Children of Dune* depicted a scene in which the character was post coital. The actor who sent it found an actress and filmed himself screaming in orgasm, before he began the scene. The director had a good laugh but the actor didn't get the role. Remember that the casting tape should be as simple as possible. You want the director to be looking at you and your raw acting ability, not your sets and costume design skills. Indeed, your tape will look amateur because you probably are an amateur when it comes to shooting. That's OK.

Do not include a scene partner

Unless you want them to be cast too, don't let your scene partner appear on your tape. The person you're reading with should be off camera. If they're a good actor, that's fine, but it's not a necessity. You run the risk that the director will become more interested in the other players rather than you. I've seen it happen. 'He's not so good but what about *her*?'

Don't worry about complicated blocking

Remember the KISS rule (keep it simple, stupid). There are all kinds of creative ways that a director may choose to shoot a scene. This does not apply to castings. Shoot yourself from the most flattering angle, but don't worry about shooting it creatively. Stick to the boring formula as described above; we'll see three quarters of your face, focused to a point near the lens most of the time.

Don't throw away the best moments in the scene

Remember that so much of acting is reacting. Sometimes it is the moments in between the text, the reaction shots, that reveal the character's inner feelings. I've seen too many casting tapes in which actors concentrate on speaking the lines rather than on reacting.

Self casting — the dos and don'ts

DO	DON'T
Start with a wide shot that shows your entire body, both profiles, and then zoom in for the introduction. Introduce yourself briefly, stating your name, height and agent	Announce your age
Keep your shots simple. Face the camera and expose at least three quarters of your face most of the time	Get fancy with editing or shooting
Have your scene partner read off screen and close to the camera lens. The camera should always be on you	Focus the camera on any actor other than yourself, unless you want to audition your scene partner as well
Use a simple background	Shoot on a location, use elaborate sets, costumes and props
Sit close to the mic or get a professional separate mic	Stand so far from the mic that your scene partner is louder on the tape then you are
Practice with several takes, but just choose one or two	Send in many takes
Send in one medium shot up (from the waist up) and close up (just face)	Show a lot of blank wall space over your head
Make sure your eyes are well lit	Sit with the window behind you

Self auditions and showreels

In discussion about self auditions and showreels, actors get confused about the difference between them. A showreel is a finished product that generally showcases an actor's work. It includes a collection of well edited scenes from a number of different projects. The reel should be professionally produced with high quality shots, whether self produced or otherwise.

A self audition is when an actor auditions for a specific role in a specific project with sides sent to her by the production. This DVD or upload may not look professional. If you can and want to hire a studio, great, but it's not necessary. The emphasis here is on the actor's interpretation of the role and the shooting should be as basic as possible with the actor clearly presented.

Things to remember from this chapter

* Own a camera and know how to use it

* Keep your shots simple and clean

* Feature your performance only

Internet casting and marketing

Online casting is at a nearly 100% saturation level for commercial submissions, 85% of TV submissions are going electronic, and about 65% of feature film projects are seeking online submissions only.

Bonnie Gillespie, Casting Director[1]

Where do you go when you want to buy or find something? You go to the internet, of course. So where do you think casting directors go when they're looking for actors? Today in casting everything happens fast, fast, fast and online. Agents submit actors electronically to casting directors, who receive hundreds of submissions in the first hour after a breakdown is posted. Almost the moment an actor auditions for me, I pop her onto a site called Castit to share with the producers and directors.

In the nineties, when cell phones were newly popular, I remember an actor's comment that, 'having a cell phone is the difference between getting the job or not'. Indeed, then as now, casting is sometimes simply about getting an actor quickly to set. Having a cell phone now is a given, so the difference between getting the job or not has more to do with internet presence. When I'm in a brainstorming session with a director, I may refer to an actor off the top of my head. If I can immediately access that actor's reel on the internet, he's that much closer to the job. Producer Fred Roos marvels that, 'The internet allows access instantly to any actor who comes into your brain at the click of a button'. When the director

---

[1] Gillespie, Bonnie. *Self-Management for Actors: Getting Down to (Show) Business.* Cricket Feet Publishing. Los Angeles, 2009.

has access to all your materials online, he's more likely to short list you for the role, quicker than the actor without the web presence. Yes, it is your agent's job to market you, but getting your own materials online makes it much easier for your agent to sell you. You're giving her the tools she needs to help you book the job.

I suggest a four-pronged strategy for internet presence.

1. Register on the major quality casting sites and databases
2. Construct and maintain a website that uniquely markets you
3. Use mailing lists and 'viral marketing' (see p. 140) to get your message out
4. Be Google-able and YouTube-able

1. Casting sites and databases

The internet offers a vast range of databases designed for actors and the entertainment business. Although I list some of the major ones here, there are hundreds more and by the time this book is published there will be new ones and the old ones will have new options and functions, so actors need to keep up with the ever-changing world.

The most ubiquitous entertainment website is the Internet Movie Data Base (IMDB: www.imdb.com) which casting directors use everyday. Serious actors should exploit all the possibilities that it offers, and join the advanced IMDB.pro, which allows you to insert contact details so that professionals can find you, and it also enables you to find them. Ensure that your current photo and CV are posted and updated on IMDB at all times. There is a special function on IMDB.pro that allows you to insert your own separate resume, that could include work that IMDB hasn't picked up.

Keeping your material updated is essential. Sometimes when an actor auditions, the director may ask me why hasn't he worked for a number of years? I then realize that the actor has been working non-stop but for some reason didn't think it was important to update his Spotlight or IMDB page to which the director is referring. Although it costs, posting your headshot on IMDB is a solid investment. Many directors rely on IMDB. When a director is looking for the actor who played the bridesmaid at the wedding, for example, how can they know which bridesmaid? With your photo posted, there's no doubt.

IMDB also provides a STARmeter ranking system based on how many hits your page gets. The lower the star meter ranking, the more noticed an actor is. It helps casting directors gauge an actor's popularity and could indicate when an actor is up and coming. While it's not a decisive factor, a good STARmeter ranking can play a role in casting decisions since the more popular an actor, the more likely an audience is to buy tickets. You can move your STARmeter rating up by adding as many links to your IMDB page as possible. Add your IMDB link to your website and in the signature of your outgoing emails. Interacting with any incoming fan mail that you receive on your message board, keeps your page active.

Casting directors don't agree about how important the STARmeter is:

> *I use it because we are very controlled by the financiers of films and we all know that we are serving 13–22 year old boys in Iowa, and we have to look at who's hot for the top of the casting. So the STARmeter is very important.*
>
> Ros Hubbard

> *It's a spurious measurement but it's measuring something. Executive gullibility? Maybe it's nervousness that it's measuring. Because the financiers have got to risk their money on this person.*
>
> Maureen Duff

> *I've been on a feature film once where the director was in love with an actor who was not right for a role and the justification for casting him in some ways was that he had the most hits on the screen, and that's where we get into a grey area. They may have super hits but if they're not suited for a role, it's not going to work.*
>
> Lucinda Syson

Here is a view from an actor who has managed to improve her STARmeter ranking:

> *I recently discovered that my website host has many different applications I can use, including an email newsletter. It's amazingly simple to use, which was important to me, and all I had to do was import my contacts from my email account. That also allowed me to track which links people clicked on. The only links I included in the newsletter were my personal website, my IMDB account, and an unsubscribe link. Only six people of the 300 I emailed actually unsubscribed, about 60 people didn't open the newsletter. But most noticeably, my IMDB ranking went from around 60,000 to 13,000 that week. Because of the big number jump, I was featured on the Fresh Faces page of IMDB.*
>
> Elaine Loh

Following is a list of major actor casting databases where smart actors maintain an active presence. There are many more sites that you can research and use at your discretion.

USA
Actors Access — actorsaccess.com
Iactor (for SAG members) — sag.org/iactor-online-casting
Now Casting — nowcasting.com
Casting About — castingabout.com

UK
Spotlight — www.spotlight.com
Casting Call Pro — castingcallpro.com
The Casting Scene — thecastingscene.com
Cast Web — www.castweb.co.uk
Shooting people (for independent projects in the US and UK) — www.shootingpeople.org

Europe

E-talenta — www.e-talenta.eu

Casting-network — www.casting-network.de

Australia

Showcast — www3.showcast.com.au

> It's employment suicide for an actor not to be on Spotlight.
>
> Frank Moiselle, Casting Director

> Because of Spotlight and the internet age, we have a lot more access to actors all over the world. We're looking for English speaking actors and that takes in Canada, Australia, US, Ireland, England. So it means the resources are larger. We have access to lots of good actors and it makes everything more immediate. Whereas we'd wait three days to transfer a casting session onto a video tape, now it's immediate because we take the casting session and upload it onto Castit immediately.
>
> Lucinda Syson, Casting Director

2. Website

Databases like Spotlight etc are essential but they are not enough. There are directors who aren't using those sites or who are looking outside the box. I believe that a website, properly designed by a professional, is a worthwhile investment.* If money is tight, I have also seen actors successfully design their own websites. It is not expensive to buy your own domain, such as www.wendywannarole.com. This gives you a professional email address such as

* I have learned from my colleagues that not all casting directors share my view that websites are important. I still maintain that even if casting directors are using the directories, there will still be 'customers' looking outside the box.

wendy@wendywannarole.com or info@wendywannarole.com, as well as your personal one. A website enables you to brand and market yourself in a unique way because you can control the content and presentation. In any campaign, the marketers will ask the following three questions first.

1. What do you do?
2. Who are your customers?
3. Why do they buy from you?

Let these marketing questions guide the content of your website.

What do you do?

Make it clear that you're a professional actor. Don't muddle the site with too many conflicting images or extra-curricular interests that could lead viewers to think that acting is a hobby. If you are expert in something else that enhances your acting, such as stunts, horse-back riding, stand-up comedy or dance, then devote some space to it. But make sure it's not too prominent or it will look like you're a stuntman or dancer before an actor.

Who are your customers?

Harrison Ford knows that he's a product. On a radio interview he referred to the audience as his 'customers'. According to talent manager Derek Power, 'You have to create a billboard for yourself. You have to market yourself. You are your own product. That means you should have a website. Treat yourself as a business with one client that has to be branded and merchandised to an audience who are casting directors, producers, directors. Ultimately they are your customers'. Figure out what information they would need to cast you. Ensure your site is usable by all customers by testing it on different browsers, such as Mac and PC, Firefox and Outlook; once I couldn't access an actor's reel on my Mac computer but because I was very interested in her, I switched to my PC and was successful, but she would have been out of the race if I had been either marginally interested or without both types of computers.

> *Working in Hollywood does give one a certain expertise in the field of prostitution.*
>
> Jane Fonda, Actor

Why should they buy from you?

Good question. There are millions of actors in the world, so what makes you special? Why should they cast you? In other words, what is the product? What are you selling? We have established that you are selling yourself. That makes it sound like prostitution doesn't it? No wonder there is a historic connection between acting and prostitution. But no, that's not quite it. You're selling your image and your range of abilities as an actor. What makes you special as an actor? Identify your image and the range of archetypes that you play. Through your personal style you will reflect, on the site, what you have to offer, how you look, what your experience is, how you've trained. 'All things spring from the client's identity,' claims web designer Deborah DeWitt, 'which incorporates, logo, logotype, fonts, colors, graphics, photos and layout. All of these combine to visually represent their offering, personality and communication style.' This design style can tie in with the design on your reel and all your presentation materials. The site expresses the predominant archetypes that you play.

> *Developing a site which reflects the individual's strengths and style is critical in having a website that stands out from the crowd. Are the roles the actor books the police officer, the CEO or the down on his/her luck struggling single parent? The website should reflect the personal style of the actor so there is no doubt in the casting director's mind, 'Yes, I can use this person for my comedy!'*
>
> Ellen Treanor Strasman, founder of Actors Webmaster

An effective actor's website will include the following:

Home page

> *Two items are paramount in web design: clarity and navigation. Your identity and message should be quickly and easily recognized within the first few seconds that someone lands on your homepage. If it isn't, most people will quickly navigate away to another site or database.*
>
> Deborah DeWitt DSW Design and Communications

The home page will prominently feature the actor's one main head shot. It's best not to muddle it with tons of different images. Save multiple photos for the gallery. Google likes changing content, so announce news like a new show or snippets of good reviews on the front page. Not only will it keep us up to date but it will make your site easier for search engines to find. You will also decide on this page what your menu items will be.

Menu items

* Resume. Here you may decide to organize your resume with selected credits as described in Chapter 16, or you may go ahead and include all your projects if you wish to have a more comprehensive list. Some actors skip the resume and link into a search engine, such as Breakdown Services or IMBD for their resume. This is handy because then they don't have to worry about updating two sites, but I would recommend posting your resume separately on the site as well. Provide downloadable and printable options to make it easier for casting directors to obtain hard copies. Make sure your contact info is on the printable copies.

* Biography. This optional heading is a short prose section that includes where you were born and how you've got to where you are now. It is a way to emphasize your background, and what makes you unique. If you escaped from war-torn Yugoslavia, for example, that could inform your experience for

a given role. If you grew up in the suburbs of New York or Manchester, it could be equally as relevant, depending on the project. The style in which the biography is written also provides an opportunity to express your personality and sense of humor.

* Gallery. Here's a chance to show the range of archetypes you can play and to offer additional information about yourself. The headshot is limited, as it is usually just that — the head. Take this opportunity to show a wider shot, so we can see your wonderfully round or modestly slim frame. If your main headshot is quite serious, but you're also good at comedy, then include a photo that reflects this side of you. If you mostly play contemporary but are also a Shakespearean trained actor, post production stills with period costume. Be selective about what images you choose, however. Web expert Ellen Treanor Strasman notes that one of the frequently made mistakes is when, 'Actors choose to put in too many photos. The average visit time per page is less than one minute so people won't look at that many photos. The rule of lists is (and this applies to the number of photos) people will look at the first three and the last one'. So put the strongest photos in these positions.

* Reel. Don't miss this part. When I'm considering an actor I don't know, I always watch their reel. There is no substitute for the moving picture. Some actors separate their work by project, showing a few clips from each. Other actors divide their clips up by type, for example, comedy, drama, action, and make mini reels. Usually actors load up their two or three minute reel (see Chapter 17). Make sure that the links work and are in a common format that viewers can watch, like Quick Time. The reel and each clip should start with your image so we're not confused about who we should be watching. If you have clips in different language, separate them.

* Press or reviews. This section will include snippets of reviews about you. You can link to the whole article or just quote one or two sentences. If you got a good notice within a bad review, feel free to pick out the phrase that flatters your performance.

* Contact. This is essential. None of the above matters if you can't be reached. If you have an agent, include all their contact details. Many casters prefer the professional distance that an agent affords. If you don't have an agent or

don't mind being contacted directly, list your own email but never post your phone number or address unless you want to invite stalkers.

Other sections that you might include are:

* Voice over. If you do voice work and have a voice reel, include that.

* Blog. This is an opportunity to express, in journal form, your own notes on projects or work. Keep it professional. No one cares about your trip to Bermuda or that your sister has just had a baby. Mention when you're doing something that expands your experience or understanding of the world, like studying tap dance or volunteering at a homeless shelter. If you like blogging about political issues or something unrelated to acting, then keep it on a separate site.

* Links. Links to and from the site are important for drawing viewers and raising your rank in search engine results. Link your page to a professional search engine, your agency or to a project you're working on, and ask them to link back to your site. The more links there are to your site, the more traffic you'll get, which will push your site to the top of the search engines.

Three top mistakes made on websites

1. Using a fancy introduction

2. Muddling your message with too many conflicting images. Know who you are, and choose only relevant images

3. Neglecting to keep your page up to date

> *The most common mistake is thinking that a site using Flash with all kinds of moving elements will be great. The fact is most people hit the 'skip intro' button; the bottom line is, content is king. Plus visitors to the site want to control their experience and Flash does not allow people to do that, it is more passive. It also hurts your chances with search engines like Google since Flash programs can't be read or catalogued.*
>
> Ellen Treanor Strasman, Actors Webmaster

Here are some suggestions from web designer Deborah DeWitt of DSW Design and Communications

You must present a compelling visual story that meets the visitor's needs in a user-friendly format that is fast and simple to digest.

Planning your website

* Collect logos and type styles that you like. Don't worry if they aren't related to acting or the film industry
* Pull out magazine ads that strike you. Illustrations, photography and artwork are also good resources
* Paint stores are a great place to look at colors. Grab your favorites in convenient sample strips
* Bookmark web sites that capture your attention, for either design or navigational organization
* Pull together examples of any designs that resonate with you — books, CD/album jackets, product packaging
* Learn about yourself in this process. Are you logical and streamlined. Is your taste leaning towards clean and striking designs? Or do you delight in fun, vibrant designs? Anything that captures your attention can be used for inspiration

Identity considerations

Your logo, stationery and marketing materials all carry both character and message to your audience. It's essential that your identity represents your product creatively, consistently and enduringly.

* Creativity. Your visual communications should be attractive, informative and compelling
* Consistency. A consistently presented identity allows for recognition and retention by customers
* Endurance. Your identity has to stand the test of time, avoiding trends or clichés.

3. Mailing list and viral marketing

> *I know that by having an online presence, it has made it easier to get auditions. My agent has told me that she will often send my link to Actors Access or Speedreels, so that people can view my demo reel and pictures. Most of the time, people are willing to at least audition me after they've viewed my material.*
>
> Elaine Loh, Actor

After this note Elaine was cast on *Curb Your Enthusiasm* without an audition!

Viral marketing sounds like something nasty, but it only means good old fashion word of mouth advertising over the internet. No one could put it better than Wikepedia: 'Viral advertising refers to marketing techniques that use pre-existing social networks to produce increases in brand awareness'. Viral marketing can happen by accident. I was attending a book festival and I wrote a simple email asking the festival where a certain venue was. Someone wrote back to me and when I got to the book signing he approached me and said, 'Are you Nancy Bishop?' How on earth did he know? Tom Dolman was the man who answered my email and he happened to click on my website which was in my web signature, saw that I was writing a book and asked me if I wanted to promote my book at the Stirling Book Festival the next year. That's an example of viral marketing. Because I had all my links embodied in my email signature, I spread the Nancy Bishop 'virus' to a potential customer.

Create mailing lists of casting directors, producers, agents and other industry professionals and judiciously send out a newsletter announcing current projects and shows. Keep a guestbook on your site for feedback, and give your viewers the opportunity to sign up for a newsletter. Newsletters keep actors in the front of our minds.

4. Be Google-able and YouTube-able

A casting director might be looking for you, but what if you're not famous? If you're shopping on the internet for a gift basket with chocolates, what do you

Google? 'Gift basket, chocolates,' right? If I'm looking for an American actor in Buenos Aires I type in 'American Actor, Buenos Aires.' Puerto Rican actor Selenia (www.selenia.tv) arrived in Los Angeles with no agent. She employed a professional web design company, Actors Webmaster, to design a snappy professional website. They developed a search engine optimization program for her to be found when someone typed in 'Spanish speaking actress, LA' and she got her first SAG job on TV series *Common Bond*, within a month of arriving in LA. An agent followed.

Think about your specific skills and what makes you unique. Use these as keys words to link to other pages on your website. The important keywords that you use should be towards the top of the page. This will help casters find you. Google needs text and key words to index and find your site. Pictures are wonderful but unfortunately Google can't index a photo, so make sure you provide alternative text under it, like 'Wendy Wannarole, Karate actor'.

> *Avoid having links that say 'click here' or similar. Google looks closely at link words and weighs them more. So rather than saying* **'Click here'** *to see my work in physical theatre', say* **'You can see samples of Wendy Wannarole's physical theatre acting here'.** *Be careful with the use of Flash. Although Flash can be useful for small bits of animation or embedded video and similar effects, it is not best for the core content of the site or the navigation. There is often a temptation to make overly 'playful' hide & seek elements on the page that are only activated by hovering over them or similar.*
>
> Chris Rourke, User Vision

I love it when I can type an actor's name into YouTube and immediately a show reel or clip surfaces. I can then paste the link into an email and send it as a suggestion to a director, or post it on Castit when I submit the actor's audition clip.

Finally, don't forget to register your site with major search engines, like Google and YouTube. They don't automatically *find* new websites; you have to register to be included in their searches.

When is marketing too much?

It's a good question without a short answer. Casting directors bemoan being harassed by actors. When I was interviewing Meg Liberman about actors using internet marketing she suggested that I talk to Elaine Loh. She said that she was an actress who was good at web marketing, but in the same breath mentioned that she was a bit irritated at receiving 'random emails from an actor', preferring them to contact her via 'the buffer of an agent or manager'. But at the same time, Elaine had made an impression and Meg knew her name. Elaine's brand it out there.

Actors can become too obsessed with their own self promotion and too many emails and newsletters can become irritating to the people who would be giving them jobs. Since there is no formula, each actor must use his discretion and exercise good taste when making choices about how, when, and how often to promote.

Moreover truth in advertising in paramount. Keep in mind the old vintner's adage 'don't sell wine before its time'. Publicists hired for promotion before an actor really has something to sell is an embarrassment. There has to be substance, not just empty marketing campaigns. Marketing and web-presence is no substitute for quality training, practice and hard work.

Things to remember from this chapter

* Casting happens quickly and primarily on the internet

* It is imperative for actors to maintain an active online presence

* Register and update often with major casting databases

* Individualize your marketing with your own website

Part 4

Perspectives from the other side of the looking glass

20 The casting director is on your side

The casting director is on your side. This may seem like a contradiction after previous chapters in which I harped on about how casting directors don't like to be contacted too much. It doesn't sound very friendly. But consider this equation:

Actors are afraid of casting directors.
Casting directors are afraid of actors.

An actor once frankly said that he was disappointed that I was so dismissive. I am sure that we do seem that way sometimes, but consider that we feel overwhelmed by actors, a bit like in the picture overleaf. Furthermore, actors who don't find success often compensate by demonizing the person who they see as the gatekeeper, standing between them and the job. We, casters, can find actors intimidating because they turn their hostility towards us. Actors are angry when they perceive themselves to be in a powerless position, and they bring their aggression with them.

While we can feel overwhelmed by actors, at the same time we need actors, good actors, to do our job. Once you've stepped into our office to audition for a role, we are one hundred percent on your side. We truly want you to be right for the role and we do everything possible to make you sparkle and shine. It doesn't always seem that way to actors, however. To them, we may seem rude, evasive or unhelpful. Try being us for a day. Here is a view from the other side of the looking glass. Consider these scenarios.

It's best to have an appointment before dropping in on a casting director

The casting director's position in the production

I was working with another casting director to cast a supporting role on a major studio production. It was a difficult role which required a very young actor who could perform physical comedy. My colleague knew the perfect actor and introduced him to the director within the first pool we presented. No matter how persuasively she tried to convince him, the director wanted us to keep looking. Five hundred actors later, she slipped this very same actor into the mix again, and the director said, 'Yes! That's him! You see what happens if you keep looking'. This story epitomizes the frustration of being a casting director. We dearly want to book the role because then our search is over, but it can be a long road until we actually get approval.

Casting directors have to play the game. Everyone who works in production — the special effects team, the costume department — has her own version of this story. Film is the director's medium. In the beginning of the film era, studios micro-managed productions, overseeing each detail, including casting, at a time when casting directors didn't even exist. In the 1960s European auteur directors started to influence American film. Studio systems gave way to directors like Francis Ford Coppola, and later Stephen Spielberg and George Lucas, who dictated the role of director as king.

In these times we still experience the deification of the director. From a casting standpoint, directors can seem unreasonably petulant and at times sociopathic, demanding more and more choices before they make a decision — like kids in a candy shop wanting to taste each lollipop before they finally choose which one. They seem to take special joy in torturing casting directors and demanding that we bring in hundreds of actors from far reaches of the earth, even when they have an excellent selection of locals in front of their faces. Brilliant actors can be overlooked because of an obstreperous director who just wants to see more, more, more.

In some productions, the studio or the network holds the balance of power more than the director. Studios sometimes hire first time directors or no-names over whom they can exercise control. In a TV series, the producer and the network have more say in casting than a director, who is usually hired freelance on an episode by episode basis. There are times when a casting director is really supportive of an actor but we may have to convince not only the director, but the producer, the executive producer, his wife, the studio casting director, the studio executive, and the network head honcho (cartoon overleaf).

More than once I have cut deals with agents, under producer and director approval, only to get a call from the studio, demanding that I retract the offer. It's embarrassing for me, and heartbreaking for the actor. Sometimes a director simply changes his mind about whom he wants to cast. Don't take it personally because it even happens to big stars. A casting director friend of mine was in the middle of negotiations when he had to call Kyle McLaughlin's agent to reverse course. Kyle McLaughlin had his day, however. Val Kilmer was promised the role of Paul Atreides in *Dune*, only to have David Lynch re-think his choice and cast McLaughlin, who was a relatively unknown Seattle theatre actor at the time. (Kilmer had already

The casting director needs approval from a diverse team

rehearsed and was suffering an eye infection from make-up tests.) Other times the director likes one actor and the producer likes another, so it becomes a political battle catapulting the casting director back to the drawing board.

Even while we support actors, we are often helpless to influence these decisions. Be assured that when you walk through the door, we want you to be the one who the director will choose. Then we can book the deal and we have succeeded in our job. Remember that we're on your side at the audition. You're the one who has the power, not us. Every actor who enters the casting room is a potential gem for us to discover. When actors nervously step in for auditions, I wonder why. Why are they nervous around me? I want them to be perfect for the role. Internalize this fact and use it as a springboard of confidence.

Don't buy into the illusion that you are a supplicant standing at the gates of success in a casting director's office. It's true that some actors view castings as capital punishment, going drearily along as if to their own executions. Don't internalize the system's hierarchy or allow casting directors and arrogant industry professionals to destroy your spirit. Believe in yourself and persevere. Director Barry Levinson recounts an early NBC pilot series called *Peeping Times*. The studio told him to get rid of one of his actors because he wasn't funny enough. It's a good thing that the actor paid no attention to the studio executives' opinion, before going on to host his own show, one of the most popular comedies in American TV history — *Late Night with David Letterman*.

What do casting directors want?

My objective is to present the director with as many brilliant, castable actors as possible. If I bring him many great actors from which to choose, then I'll look good and we'll cast the film. What do casting directors want? We want the same thing that actors want. We want more jobs on more films. The more we're able to impress the director, the more jobs we'll get. If the actor succeeds in the casting, then so do we.

We are under pressure to present great talent to a diverse panel of difficult professionals who compose the production team. We want that panel to like the actors we bring, so we work hard to present the actor in the best light possible. That is why we give directions. Listen and really take in our notes, because we're trying to help you. When I was working for Fox Studio they sent out a memo to the casting directors on the project:

> The audition is a tool to get the actor a job.
> The taped audition is a mini commercial for the actor.
> If the audition and taping session doesn't properly sell the actor for the role, there is a problem.

The studio is on your team too. The studio wants the actor auditions to be as good as possible.

On nervous directors

Actors focus on their own nervousness at auditions. Consider that the casters might be even more nervous.

The casting director is stressed because she may have two hundred people to see in two days. The director is nervous because he's got a producer breathing down his neck, and a multi-million dollar production on his shoulders. Some directors feel awkward around actors. I worked with one director who felt much more comfortable meeting with the special effects department (where he started his career) than he did meeting talent. He went out of his way to avoid actors, interrupting casting sessions so that he could show me trailers of his last film. During his sessions with actors, he didn't have the slightest idea what to say to them or how to direct them, since acting was so far from his area of expertise.

Actors in my casting workshops often tell me nightmarish stories about rude, disrespectful casting directors. I've heard stories about directors ignoring actors or taking phone calls during the audition. One actor told me that the casting director's phone was ringing during her entire casting. She asked me what she should have done. I advised her that next time she might say something like, 'That was distracting for me. May I go again?' Another actor complained how the director scowled during his entire performance. Remember, he may not be thinking about you at all. He could be thinking about the fight he had with his wife that morning. Don't let someone else's stress set you off.

Realize that there may be one hundred actors who audition for a given role. Only one will get it but that doesn't mean that the other ninety nine were poor actors. You may have done a perfectly good audition, but because of the political battles that rage in any production, you didn't get the role. If you felt that the director liked you, then it may be true, but you didn't get the role because the producer wanted his nephew to play it. Don't take anything personally, and move on.

Things to remember from this chapter

* The casting director is on the actor's side

* The casting director wants the same thing actors do — more work on more films

* Casting directors do everything possible to make actors shine

* The casting director has her own stress that might make it seem like she's not on the actor's side

* There are political battles raging on many productions that are beyond the actor's control

21

Showbiz ain't fair

Showbiz just ain't fair. It is wildly random, arbitrary and unfair.

In the British mini series, *Zhivago*, starring Keira Knightley, we needed an actor to play a one-armed, one-legged Russian soldier. After an exhaustive search, my associates and I proudly presented a one-armed, one-legged, Russian speaking actor to the director, sure that he would be happy. On top of the tough requirement, we even thought the candidate could act pretty well. When the director saw the tape, he confounded all our expectations, exclaiming, 'No! No! No! He's wrong for it'.

I was thinking, 'Why? Is the wrong leg missing?'

'He looks like he was born that way! We need someone who was amputated!' he shouted.

Sometimes an actor can do a perfectly good audition but he simply doesn't have what the production is looking for. Certain roles have physical requirements. Actors can't get plastic surgery (or amputated limbs) each time they're up for a part. This actor did a good audition but he didn't match the physical requirements of the role. Although it was shocking to me that the director put such fine a point on it, his prerogative is to be picky. It wasn't the actor's fault. There was nothing he could have done better. In the same way, you might feel that you were fantastic in the audition but still didn't succeed. What did you do wrong? Very possibly — nothing.

When I first started out, someone told me that talent always rises to the top, but after years of experience, I don't believe it's true anymore. I meet many, many talented actors to whom I cannot offer roles. Why? Because acting is the only art form in which the artist is the product. A painter can pour her soul into a painting but the piece is still a physically separate entity from her body. You would never, for example, resist buying a painting because the painter is too short.

Conversely, there are many untalented actors who do get cast. It's hurtful for trained actors to live in a world dominated by reality TV. Some directors lean towards hiring amateurs in an effort to bring authenticity to their films. When I was casting *Everything is Illuminated*, although I found plenty of trained actors, director Liev Schreiber wanted to cast real Ukrainian ditch diggers for one scene. I had to go out on the building sites and find Ukrainian workers, and he loved them for their authentic look and imperfect teeth. He didn't seem to mind their inexperience or the faint whiff of alcohol that entered the casting room with them. A trained, professional actor just can't compete in those situations.

Sometimes actors do or don't get cast for silly, non-artistically motivated reasons. Once I worked on a production in which a very short actor got cut out of a scene, simply because the director couldn't fit him into the same shot with the star, the tall Richard E. Grant. Even more often it happens the other way. On *Hellboy*, we were encouraged to find supporting cast members who were under 5¢9¢¢ because we had to make Ron Pearlman, playing Hellboy, look like a giant. Similarly on *Blade II*, we were discouraged from casting tall actors, for fear of dwarfing Wesley Snipes. The taller actors were rejected — it had nothing to do with talent.

Casting director Maureen Duff claims that when she's casting a leading lady, she tries to find out what the director's mother is like and to cast someone who is similar to her. But what if the director doesn't like his mother? So that could mean:

Reason you get cast: you look like the director's mother.
Reason you do not get cast: you look like the director's mother.

The casting process is filtered through whatever unique and unpredictable personal biases a particular director may have. We all possess certain personal qualities. These qualities may be physical — a dimpled chin or thin lips — or they may be an indescribable part of our chemistry. Michael Chekhov referred to this as creative individuality: 'To create by inspiration one must become aware of one's own individuality'.[1] But because the director also has a creative individuality through which he filters the actor's performance, he might have an

[1] Chekhov, Michael. *To the Actor on the Technique of Acting*. Harper and Row, New York, 1953.

association (positive or negative) for that actor's qualities. Danish director Ole Christian Madsen says that in casting you're often 'trying to find someone like yourself, and when you find them you want to cast them again and again'.

In other words, it has to do with personal taste. Acting coach Bernard Hiller makes the analogy of an ice cream cone — you might be pistachio but the director is allergic to nuts.

> There must be as many Hamlets as there are talented and inspired actors to undertake their conceptions of the character. The creative individuality of each will invariably determine his own unique Hamlet.
>
> Michael Chekhov[2]

Even acting skill turns out to be a matter of taste. I introduced an actor named David to a director who thought he was a terrible actor. Yet when I introduced David to a different director she thought he was brilliant.

Jiri Machacek is a well known actor in the Czech Republic. I introduced him for a role in *Anne Frank: The Whole Story* and director Robert Dornhelm told me that he was a good actor but too much like a Russian gangster to fit into the film. Shortly after, I was casting, *Black Sheep*, where we needed Russian gangsters so I thought, 'Perfect, I'll bring in Jiri Machacek'. Director Joel Schumacher simply said, 'Oh, he's too nice to play a gangster'. So it only goes to show that everyone is screening through their own particular tint of glasses.

These things are personal, but don't take them personally. It matters very little what one person in the industry thinks about you, because everyone's opinion is different anyway. If a director insults you (it happens) develop a thick skin and move on. Do what Meryl Streep did, as reported to me by a *Variety* journalist I know. While in a casting, a famous Italian director turned to the casting director and said in Italian, 'Why do you keep showing me these ugly actresses?' Although Streep understood him, she kept her chin up, completed her audition and then made sure she chatted with him in Italian before she left the room.

---

[2] Ibid.

In times of equal opportunity, there is no other profession that could get away with this kind of discrimination on the basis of physical looks. This has always been part and parcel of the casting process. When we cast a kid, meant to be the younger version of a character, then they have to look like the star; at other times we may have to cast someone who is a mother to another character so they have to look like they could be related. This is good casting, when a family fits together in a convincing way. If you were close but didn't quite make it, this may be the reason you didn't get the job.

When you audition, believe in yourself, in your own creative individuality. You don't have any control over these production factors, including what the director is thinking. Surrender to it and know that even if you don't book the job, that if you work hard and perform well, you may get a role on the next project. You are building a relationship each time you come to the casting.

It's not always about being the most attractive and sexy person around. Unless you're auditioning for *Baywatch*, this is unlikely to be the case. 'You're not pretty enough to be James Dean and you're not ugly enough to be a character actor. So forget about being an actor.' This is what legendary director Billy Wilder said to Billy Bob Thornton while he was waiting tables at a Hollywood party, years before Thornton became the movie star that he is today. 'Do you write at all?' Wilder asked. Thornton replied that yes he did write. 'Then that's what you need to do,' continued Wilder. 'Create your own way. Don't wait around. Be an innovator and originator.'

What can we learn from Wilder's early advice to Thornton? First, anyone can be a film actor regardless of how they look. Michael Shurtleff in his book *Audition*, reports the producer's first reaction to Barbra Streisand at a casting: 'She sings great, but what can we do with a girl who looks like that?'[3] If you want to be an actor, don't let anyone tell you that you're not pretty enough, ugly enough, tall or short enough. Of course Wilder was wrong about Billy Bob Thornton, so it's a good thing that Thornton didn't stop working at an acting career. Thornton took Wilder's advice, however, and didn't sit around and wait for the phone to ring. He played mostly bit parts until his breakthrough film *One False Move*, in 1992 which not coincidentally, he wrote too.

Early in my life, I decided not to be a career actor. Ironically it was partly because of early encounters with casting directors. When I was attending the National Theatre Institute, part of the program included seminars by lead casting directors from New York City. Typically they were casting soap operas and sported nasty attitudes. They were older mink clad ladies, draping little dogs on their arms. I remember hearing, 'Look, if you're fat, lose the weight; if you've got a big nose, get a nose job'. I ran away. I hope that no one who is reading my book is running out and getting a nose job or a boob job or any kind of job other than an acting job. If your hair is getting grey, please let it. It's getting harder and harder to find anyone to play the older roles because of our youth-obsessed culture.

When I cast *Oliver*, Roman Polanski wanted people who he considered to be Dickensian looking. That meant he preferred actors with crooked teeth, warts and wrinkles. The white-toothed models were sent away. When I was casting, *Anne Frank: The Whole Story*, I needed kids to play victims in the concentration camp. Parents were contacting me and bragging about their beautiful children. Little did

---

[3] Shurtleff, Michael. *Audition: Everything an Actor Needs to Know to Get the Part.* Walker and Company. New York, 1978.

they know that beauty was the last thing we wanted on this film. I needed decrepit, unhealthy, malnourished-looking kids to play scabies patients.

Actors must at times let go of vanity. I was once offered the role of an Edwardian era landlady on *From Hell*, a Jack the Ripper thriller, starring Johnny Depp. When I got to set, they sent me to make-up where they first covered my skin in pale foundation, then smeared on black gunge. They proceeded to distress my teeth with a waxy brown paste. Not content with my ugliness, they continued to smear grease in my hair and knot it up. The costume department found a wrinkled old black dress, and when I got to set, a skinny cat was thrust into my arms and he promptly peed on me. At that moment I was introduced to Mr. Depp — and it wasn't exactly my dream scenario. Around that time I realized that I wasn't hired for my looks. Sometimes if you understand this before you go to the casting, it can help you a lot. (By the way, don't look for me in *From Hell*. The scene was cut, at the last minute apparently, according to the Hughes brothers. Did I say anything about the movie business being unfair?)

Things to remember from this chapter

* Showbiz ain't fair

* Physical discrimination is a normal part of casting

* Much of casting is determined by the actor's and the director's creative individuality

* Talent doesn't always rise to the top

* Actors need to let go of vanity

22

Perspectives from casting directors around the world

The following notes are collected from various casting symposiums that I've panelled.

For non-American actors who want to work in the US

The United States is not the only place in the world for actors to work, and it's not even the largest film industry, with both Europe and India surpassing it in the number of films produced per year. Yet Hollywood continues to be the goal for actors from many countries. Many international actors we know, like Karel Roden from the Czech Republic, Mads Mikkelsen from Denmark, and Juliette Binoche from France, made their name at home first, fast tracking themselves into the American market. International actors geared towards the hyper-competitive American scene must have stamina, passion and break-back perseverance. They also need to confront the bureaucratic process of applying to work in the US.

British actor Ian McNeice jokes about his status in America: 'I'm an alien of extraordinary ability'. It's another way of saying that he has an 0-1 visa, which is the legal documentation that a non-resident must obtain to work in the United States. The 0-1 is specifically designed for 'foreign nationals of extraordinary ability in the arts . . . or motion picture or television industry'. Essentially the artist must petition for this visa, proving that they are an expert in their field. Expertise is determined by awards, and documentation of critical and/or commercial success. Letters of recommendation from industry professionals such as casting directors, producers or directors corroborate an actor's standing and strengthen the application. A successful application will require time, money and a good American lawyer. There are many firms that specialize in smoothing the process. A manager on the US side is another essential asset.

English speaking actors from around the world

The International Alliance of Casting Directories (IACD), a global organization, has made it possible for casting directors to coordinate talent in North America, the UK, Australia, New Zealand, and South Africa. Thanks to online networks such as Breakdown Services and Spotlight, casting directors anywhere in the world can post their breakdowns and get submissions internationally. When you are cast in an American project through this system, normally production will take care of your working papers.

Australia has proven to be extremely strong in American films, with actors like Nicole Kidman, Russell Crowe, Cate Blanchet and Geoffrey Rush to name only a few. LA agents and managers routinely go to Sidney to cherry pick clients from drama schools there. The Australians have a good facility to pick up American accents.

British actors are managing to stay at home and still break into the American scene, as the American Networks and Studios search globally. London casting director Suzanne Smith is known for casting British talent in American roles, like Michelle Ryan as *The Bionic Woman*. Surely she was competing against many American actors. 'I believe that Brits bring a cerebral quality,' says Smith. 'With Michelle Ryan she had the girl next door quality they were looking for.' British actors are in fact excelling in American projects, often playing in American accents. Examples include Kate Winslett, Eddie Izzard, Ciaran Hinds, Alfred Molina, Lena Heady, Matthew Rhys, Hugh Laurie (from *House MD*). 'Hugh had everything they wanted — humor, depth,' says Smith. Though she added that he had to really work his American accent.

> *Remember we have a theatre tradition: theatre adds weight and levels to performances. We do so many*

*American plays in England. Arthur Miller previewed many
of his plays here before New York. We have a long
history of Brits playing Americans. For example Laurence
Olivier, Cary Grant, James Mason. Vivien Leigh was the
Brit who got the role of Scarlet in* Gone with the Wind —
everyone was tested in the USA. There's nothing new
about it.

Suzanne Smith, Casting Director

Actors from smaller countries

If you do decide to leave your country and work in America or Britain, you need
to learn to break out of your accent and adapt yourself to the new culture. Don't
lose your specific ethnic identity, however. It can be very valuable as a branding
device. One Greek actor complained that he would be typecast if he worked in
America. Typecasting means *casting*, I pointed out. In America or the UK, he
could use his 'Greekness' to brand himself, while if he chose to stay in Greece,
he would just be another Greek actor.

At a casting symposium at the Berlinale Talent Campus, an actress from
Lebanon stood up and asked, 'Since I come from a region in crisis, and since
cinema is practically non-existent in our country . . . What are the chances and
opportunities for an actor from the Middle East to be cast for a film on an
international or European level?' On the same day, a Croatian actress asked a
similar question.

Whenever a region experiences war or crises, it becomes the subject of
epic story-telling, in films and TV series. Actors from places like the former
Yugoslavia and the Middle East can take advantage of their position. Productions
are frequently looking for actors from these regions and because film demands
authenticity, casters love finding the real thing — actors who have really
experienced the subject matter. I was very pleased to cast Albanian and
Serbian actors on the Kosovo episode of *The Philanthropist* TV series. The
problem for casting directors is *finding* this talent, because often the infrastructure
isn't organized enough for agents to emerge. In these regions actors do best
to form collectives, posting their credentials on the web. This would have
helped Leo Davis tremendously when she was casting *The Constant Gardener*

in Kenya. She needed to find native actors there and was finally able to locate a remote theatre in Nairobi where she cast eight actors from a production of *Othello*.

> *Get an agent outside of your country. One time an American casting director contacted us and wanted to cast Arab actors on a production . . . Big production companies call American and European casting directors to then go to those countries so you should get in contact with casting directors and get registered on databases outside of the country.*
>
> Beatrice Kruger, founder of E-Talenta, Rome

> *I know an English actor with Italian parents and he kept getting the role of the Italian waiter in London. Then he went to LA and thought he'd get gangster films, but now he's in Rome and because he's such a fluent English speaker, he's getting cast in Rome on American films shot there because he's a really good actor. He just couldn't quite work out where he should be.*
>
> Maureen Duff, Casting Director, London

What about foreign names?

Many actors who want to work in the English-language market wonder if they should change or Anglicize their names. There is no clear answer. At a casting symposium in Dublin, an Irish actress with a long difficult to pronounce last name asked if she should change it. Irish casting director Frank Moiselle advised, 'The American casting directors will get embarrassed if they can't pronounce the name and they'll move on. It's as simple as that and it's terribly unfair'. If you do decide to change your name remember that you should do it as early in your career as possible. Once your credits are listed under one name, they will be invisible under your new name. It's true that Americans are not good at languages and when immigrants arrived at Ellis Island, names were shortened inadvertently. If you do want to keep your name and identity, however, I encourage it. Remember that we all learned to say Schwarzenegger.

What about the accent?

While your accent may be precisely why you are being cast, it can be very hard for English speaking audiences to understand a foreign accent. I have known foreign actors who learned the American accent so well that they've actually had to re-learn their native accent. Even for those who speak English as a first language, regional dialects can be a problem on the broader market. Scottish actor James MacAvoy has been successful in part because he can drop his Glaswegian accent so easily and pick up a British or American one.

Lina Todd, based in New York, said, 'I think it's great to keep your identity and your look, but you should perfect your English if you want to give yourself more opportunity to get a wider range of roles'.

Emma Style from London advised, 'Work on your accents in English because particularly in America, they find it hard to understand accents. So before you want to crack the English or American market, get yourself a voice coach to help you so your accent is not so strong'.

'If you do go elsewhere, you have to stop being a Scottish actor or you just get typecast, "Oh, there's Tom, he's Scottish. Give the role to Tom". I know I've got a file in the office called hidden Scots. They'll come in and I'll say, "I never knew you were Scottish" and I'll get a family history; it's exactly the same with Irish actors. You can't be in London and get typecast as an Irish actor', said John Hubbard.

Anja Dihrberg from Berlin said, 'Make a short interview [in English] on your show reel, so a director can hear your accent because that is the most important thing for English and foreign directors … They need to hear how good your English is before they can call you in for a reading'.

Cultural differences in the casting room

European actors sometimes find American directors abrupt. While working with Joel Schumacher, we scheduled ten minutes with each actor, but he consistently only saw actors for less than five minutes and everyone felt dismissed. I asked casting directors to comment on different directorial styles.

'I once worked with an American director and I was shocked because he asked me to arrange appointments for each person to have four minutes and I just couldn't do it because in Italy people always tend to come late . . . and they are very upset if the audition goes short . . . But this director saw everybody in two and a half minutes. He was so concentrated that he saw exactly what he wanted in those two and a half minutes. So you have to respect that too. It's a different way of working', observed Beatrice Kruger from Rome.

Dublin based Amy Rowan said, 'It seems to me that American directors just want to get on with business. It's very quick because normally they're very experienced. They don't want to have any kind of small talk beforehand'.

'Every director is different,' said Anja Dihrberg. 'I also know German directors who don't need to talk to actors, and just want to have a quick interview. Others like to talk, whether they be English or French or American. So I don't notice a cultural difference'.

Lina Todd said, 'Some directors like to play with the actor, and some want to do it once and then the actor feels like they've done an awful job . . . An actor should never feel that because a director spends less time with them . . . that . . . it's really a reflection of whether or not they're going to get the part'.

'Somebody like Franco Zeffirelli can spend two hours while making soup talking to an actor, or he can spend five minutes,' said Emma Style. But she added, even when he spends two hours, the actor might not get the part.

Copenhagen-based Rie Hedegaard said, 'I do a lot of work with the actors, which means I have a lot of influence. So I work with them for at least one and a half hours'.

On culture and dressing

'I realized differences when casting with German, American or French directors, as opposed to Italian directors,' said Beatrice Kruger, founder of E-Talenta in Rome. 'For often an English director will say "Wow! The women here, they all come dressed up as if they're going out to eat a man". They all come in painted, with stockings and high heels, very sexy. And it's true that Italian actresses are dressed up, on the vamp side . . . because their agents tell them that and because Italian men and directors like that. I find that when I go to an audition in England that it's very normal that all the actresses come in with just simple white t-shirts and torn jeans, and then the Italian directors say, "Oh, they didn't even dress up for me". So you have two mentalities and maybe a German uptight director (because this happened too) will say, "What does she want from me? Why did she dress up like that?" And I'll say, "She didn't want anything from you. That's just the way it is". This is also an expression of the richness of European cultures.'

Cornelia Von Braun who works in Munich remarked, 'I don't really care how they come into a casting, but I personally feel it helps if you're going for a period role to wear a certain collar or a suit or something that will make you carry yourself differently. You don't have to act *over* the t-shirt. You don't have to play the suit, if you're wearing a suit'.

Anja Dihrberg said, 'If the costume becomes more important than the acting, then we have a problem, of course. We don't want an actor to come with a suitcase and say "I can wear this or that, etc", it drives you crazy'.

Emma Style observed, 'British actors often come in with their hair uncombed and looking scruffy'.

On typecasting

Beatrice Kruger maintained, 'We cannot deny that there is typecasting for the pure reason that it's not just the actor's personality but also the director's'.

Lina Todd said, 'I think that the most important thing is talent ... To limit [actors] in one way or another is dull, uninteresting and does not make for an exciting film. I think that people often run into directors who have a vision that the character is blond and blue-eyed or this and that, and can't get that vision out of their head until an actor who's African American and the complete opposite physically comes in and is so right that you just feel it ... Because it's actors who bring the pages of the script to life ... It helps if they can feel the character internally rather than externally'.

Lilia Trapani from Rome said, 'I think the aim of the actor should be a different type in every movie she does'.

'I think it's really our [the casting director's] job to go to the theatre, see what that actor is able to do,' said Patricia Vasconcelos based in Lisbon, and then to challenge them by offering another type of role entirely. 'This is what I think is more interesting in our job.'

Conclusion

We can conclude that actors are working in a globalized market, which makes the possibilities more exciting than ever. Make the best of your marketing opportunities on the internet and value your assets as a unique artist from a specific place on the globe. See the big picture. Think broad and outside the box. Casting directors are.

Things to remember from this chapter

* Moving to Los Angeles is not the only choice for actors

* Non-resident actors who wish to work in the US need an 0-1 visa

* Casting is global in these times, with productions doing world-wide searches for talent

* Keep your national identity, but perfect your English in different dialects to open yourself to as many markets as possible

Part 5

Practical
exercises

Your camera and you

A camera is a necessary investment for anyone interested in screen acting. For those who were taught the inside out method of acting, watching our performance from the outside can be off-putting and painful. Indeed, Stanislavski warned his students, 'You must be very careful in the use of a mirror. It teaches an actor to watch the outside rather than the inside of a role'.[1] In the early stages of learning film acting however, I believe that actors must get to know themselves on screen. It's necessary to see when an eyebrow goes astray or know when one is bouncing out of frame. In front of camera, actors can rehearse auditions and practice the techniques of screen acting. The camera is essential for discovering that middle ground that balances the artist between over-acting (doing too much) and dead face (doing nothing.) We talk about naturalism but honestly there is nothing natural about acting on stage or on camera. In this section I suggest exercises for use in class or on your own.

While these exercises are helpful for the process of learning screen acting, it is ultimately important, however, not to become self obsessed. When filming you need an outside person, like a director, to direct your performance and ensure that your work fits with the whole. In a production situation, trust the director. Directors will not stand for actors who run to the monitor after each shot and demand a re-take if they're not satisfied.

Exercise 1. Warm up

What do you do before you go on stage or on camera? For every actor it's different. Some actors jump up and down, some sing while others do yoga. Figure out what *you* need to do for yourself to perform well. In acting classes, the class warms up. At an audition no one will warm you up and you may

[1] Stanislavski, Konstantin. Translated by Elizabeth Reynolds Hapgood. *An Actor Prepares*. Routledge, 1948.

only get one take so you have to be warm from the start. The problem is do you feel comfortable warming up in the reception room before the audition? Probably not. Here's an exercise to be done in a chair, based on the teachings of Alexander.

Frederick Alexander 1869–1955

Alexander was an actor who developed a system of physical exercises to alleviate tension. His technique was based on the theory that stress in the body can inhibit the flow of emotions. Actors tend to push to manipulate a performance, creating tension in the body. Stress in not a problem; the actor's creativity comes in the way he reacts to and manages the stress. If an actor holds tension in his neck, for example, it will constrict the voice. These are the actor's reactions, not the characters. Therefore the actor must be in a relaxed state to perform well. Alexander Technique teaches actors a way to organize, be aware of and manage body tension, directing it towards character not towards interference with performance.

You can practice this relaxation exercise in a chair, without making a fool of yourself in the reception room.

Place your feet flat on floor.
Ensure that you are well balanced on your sitting bones.
Sit on the edge of the chair.
Concentrate on breathing deeply.
Concentrate on lengthening the spine in two directions.
Visualize your head posed at the top of your spine.
Visualize your torso lengthening and widening.
Concentrate internally on this mantra: 'Let my neck be free, to let my head go forward and up, to let my torso lengthen and widen, to let my legs release away from my torso and to let my shoulders widen.'

Imagine a ball of energy moving from your toes to your ankles, to your shin, thighs, and buttocks. Visualize the energy moving through each part of your body, including the torso, the hips, and all your joints. Include your neck, shoulders and facial muscles. Relaxing the jaw and throat is important for vocal relaxation.

Once you have isolated each body part through the relaxation, gradually allow each vertebra in your back to collapse, with your head leading your torso into a forward bend. Your torso moves as a unit from the hip sockets.

Then allow your head to lead your torso up so that you are vertical again.

Clear your mind, take a breath, and concentrate on the choices you have made for the character. Run the lines in your head. Step in for your audition.

Exercise 2. Blank scenes

I call these scenes blank because the actor needs to fill in the blanks; we know nothing about the characters — who they are, where they are or what their motives are. Famous Russian actor and teacher, Michael Chekhov, devised blank scenes such as these for his technique so they are sometimes called Chekhovians. I use them in my casting workshops because they are excellent exercises to practice making choices. Practicing a blank scene is not unlike doing an audition for a film. Often you haven't read the script and know very little about the character, so you have to make choices. Practice these scenes with a partner. Make specific choices, based on answering the following questions.

* Who am I?

* Where am I?

* Who am I talking to?

* What do I want?

* What are the stakes?

* Where are the changes?

Blank scene 1

A: I can't believe it's been so long.
B: Good things are worth waiting for.
A: You look great.

B: You look the same.

A: The same?

B: Yeah, it's a compliment

A: I can't stand this any more.

B: Stand what.

A: Where did you put it?

B: Put what?

A: Don't play games with me.

B: You haven't changed a bit have you? Just forget it.

A: You can't just leave me here.

B: Me? Leave you?

Blank scene 2

A: Hi.

B: Hello.

A: What's up?

B: What do you mean?

A: Just what's up? Just making conversation.

B: Where were you?

A: Out.

B: What do you mean, 'out'?

A: Just out, that's all.

B: Right.

The possibilities are endless for these scenes. Experiment with playing each scene three different ways, as you would during the casting. As a warm up, play off camera with your partner. Then take turns in front of camera. You will have to agree what the relationship is between you and decide where you are. You don't have to share your objective; that can be secret.

Then ask your partner to read off-screen in a neutral voice, giving no energy (as you might get at a casting), and focus the camera on your face. Rise to the challenge of making specific, actable choices without getting inspiration or energy from the other actor.

Exercise 3. Listening and the inner monologue

In front of the camera, listening and reacting can be even more important than speaking. When I'm casting a supporting role with few lines, it's often hard to find dialogue where the character speaks several lines consecutively. So I keep the camera on the actor while I speak all of the other lines. These types of roles present an even bigger challenge to actors than a character who speaks all the time. The actor has to be constantly on, engaged in an ongoing inner monologue or soundtrack of thoughts, listening and reacting to all of the actions and speech of the characters around him.

I like to challenge actors by giving them scenes with few lines because it shows the director that the actor has the skill to be featured in a reaction shot. On a TV set there may be five cameras shooting at the same time, catching every character's reaction. If your reactions and listening skills are not up to par, you'll get less screen time. Michael Caine, in *Acting in Film*, discusses how surprised he was when he started working in Hollywood with actors like Sylvester Stallone who wanted to cut his own lines. Caine came from a theatre background where everyone wanted as many lines as possible. It was because Stallone realized that the most interesting moments are in the silences, not in the speech.

The following exercises, to be done in partners or in a classroom, are designed to develop the listening and inner monologue skills that are imperative in a casting as well as on set. In castings, so often actors throw away their silences and reactions by reading the other character's lines instead of listening. When an actor reads the lines, we only see their eyelids and the top of their head.

Take 1. Medium shot

Actor B stands off camera and tells a story (see the example below). The camera shoots Actor A who is listening in a medium frame. The featured actor does not speak but merely listens and reacts silently. It is best to choose a story that will impact the actor who is listening. Here's an example: Actor A (the featured, listening actor) is a nightclub owner and Actor B is the manager.

Actor B says (this can be improvised): 'I'm sorry, but I have to tell you something difficult and I'm glad you're sitting down. Last night at the club there was a loose wire behind the DJ equipment and it caught fire. We tried to use the extinguishers but the fire still got out of control and by the time the fire department came, well, it was too late. You've lost everything. The club is gone. The good news is that no one was hurt and everyone had a great time raiding the bar during the pandemonium. Sorry about the ninety year old bottle of Scotch.'

Take 2. The Less is More Theory
Shoot in close up.

This time Actor B can tell the same story or a different story (something that impacts Actor A). Actor A will listen, again being mindful of the fact that this is a close up. In my class, I ask how the acting changes in a close up shot. The class will often answer that less is more, and that the acting should be smaller. The camera is right there so it will pick up everything. Thinking is enough for the camera. So in Step 2, Actor A will go with the theory that less is more, and keep his reactions contained and smaller than in life.

Take 3. The More is More Theory
Shoot in close up again, and Actor B will tell the same story.

Some actors believe that an actor does more in a close up. Patrick Tucker, in *Secrets of Screen Acting*, argues that in a close up, 'You sometimes need to do more than you would ever do in real life or on the stage, because the only acting instrument you have for this shot is your face, and it has to do what you would normally use your whole body to do'. So this time, Actor A will test Mr. Tucker's theory, listening and reacting more intensely in the face.

Take 4. The Harbor a Secret Theory
Keep the camera in close up.

This time, as Actor A is listening to Actor B's story, he will concentrate on playing contrast in his inner monologue. How to play contrast? There are times when someone tells us something and we don't want them to know how we feel. This can be achieved when Actor A has a secret. Imagine a poker game. Keeping a secret is an effective choice because often we want to keep our cards close to our chest. For example, he could choose to be happy that the club burned down because he wants to collect insurance. Maybe he set fire to it himself. In any case, Actor A is likely to give a more complex performance on the screen this time.

Take 1

Were you really listening?

Did it *look like* you were really listening?

If you were the director, would you want to feature this actor in a reaction shot?

The first take is probably the easiest in terms of really listening because you've never heard Actor B's story before, but is really listening interesting to watch on camera? Sometimes our faces are blank when we're listening. This could be OK, if the character is deliberately playing a poker face. Or it may be boring. You might have to consider other techniques.

Take 2

Is it effective to contain your expressions and reactions?

Does this create a believable performance?

If you were a director, would you want to feature this actor in close up?

Is it under-played?

Is it over-played?

Some people naturally have expressive faces and large reactions. If you are one of these people, then you may well have to concentrate on limiting your facial expressions and learn to develop stillness, keeping the reactions and inner monologue in the eyes and not in the face. Some unconsciously direct their responses into an overly scrunched forehead. (I have heard of acting teachers who suggest putting masking tape on the forehead to break the habit.) New actors invariably think that film acting is about doing nothing. Doing nothing, however, often results in that dead face. Watch for it.

Take 3

Was the face alive?

Was the performance interesting and engaging?

Was the screen filled with information?

If you were a director would you want to feature this actor?

Was the performance too over the top or at the right level?

What actors learn from this exercise is that you can get away with a lot more than they think they can. Theatre actors come with the impression that film acting is 'smaller' or less exaggerated than theatre acting, so they're terrified of over-acting and they end up with a performance that is frankly boring and flat on screen. Other actors may watch take three and realize that for them, less *is* more. For actors who are naturally animated, reacting more intensively in the face might cause them to jump out of the screen. Actors new to film acting need to experience this process of experimentation to learn what level is right for them.

Take 4

Did the actor play contrast in his reactions?
Was the screen filled with information?
Was this performance more effective than the previous takes?
Was keeping a secret effective?

The camera loves contrast and variety. The camera also loves mystery and secrets. An actor who has an active and complex inner monologue is likely to have the most compelling performance. When you have a long reaction shot, the worst this you can do is to react in only one way.

I throw this last direction out to actors in my workshop for a bit of fun. Each time the experiment is different. Quite often, hard math problems upset actors so it will give them a perplexed and unpleasant look on their face while they are trying to solve the problem. Other times, it doesn't work at all because it's clear that the actor is not reacting to the specific points in the monologue. Very often, however, we can see the wheels turning in the actor's head, which can be quite engaging. On occasion the class has agreed that it's an extremely compelling performance (while not knowing what the actor was actually thinking because I give the direction secretly). The reason I toss this take into the mix is to demonstrate the Whatever Works Theory. It only matters what works on screen. If doing a math problem will work for your character in a particular reaction shot then go for it!

Exercise 4. 'Over there!' — Playing with the eyes

This exercise draws from Commedia dell'Arte techniques originated by Tim Robbins' theatre company, the Actors' Gang. This exercise is intended to help actors practice and develop their ability to communicate feelings through the eyes. The Actors' Gang, inspired by the teaching of George Bigot of Cirque du Soliel, developed a style based on the actor being 'stated' in one of the four primary emotions — sadness, anger, happiness or fear. That means that the actor finds inspiration that will crank him into an optimum high intensity of emotion. On a scale from one to ten, the actor plays a ten. He then brings that emotion with him to play objectives in the scene.

In this style of theatre, the actor must at all times be heightened in one of these emotional states and send it out through the eyes, making contact with the audience. I adapted this approach to a film acting exercise called Over There. In film you can't connect with the audience so you have to connect with an image near the camera lens.

Set up the camera and mark a spot next to it at eye level. The actor steps in front of camera, points at the spot and says, 'Over there'. She does this four times, once each for the four emotions listed above. The first time she is pointing to something that is incredibly sad. She must imagine the saddest thing in the world to her, her dead child or burned down home, etc. The second time it will be something that makes her incredibly happy like her soldier husband, thought dead, returning home safely. The actor continues through this process, pointing to something that makes her angry, then something that prompts fear.

Watch the tape and evaluate:

Was the actor at a heightened state of emotion? If you were measuring on a scale of one to ten, was she all the way at a ten?
Did the actor communicate clearly with her eyes?
What does the actor need to work on to improve communicating with the eyes?

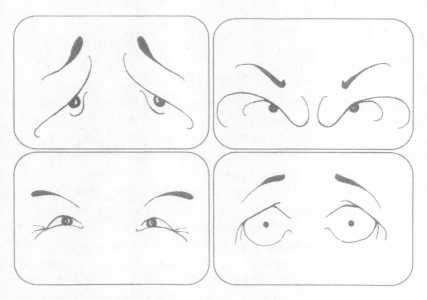

Figure. V.1. The four emotions

I realize that there is a contradiction in this exercise. I have spent a whole book emphasizing the point that actors need to play action, not emotion. Now here's an exercise that is all about playing emotion. This 'stated' sense of awareness can be applied to a scene in which there is an objective. I could see this training in Tim Robbins' performance in *The War of the Worlds* in which he played a petrified homeowner cowering in his basement, while terrifying aliens invade Earth. He was in a permanent sense of fear that riddled his eyes and body, while at the same time playing the objective to fight for survival.

Exercise 5. Playing the objective

The following are examples of strong objectives. Note that they all take direct objects, eg 'to seduce him'.

* To challenge
* To convince
* To change

* To avenge
* To hurt
* To amuse

* To tease

* To undress

* To scare

* To arouse

* To irritate

* To forgive

* To scold

* To placate

* To motivate

* To punish

* To shame

* To shag

* To change

Choose from the list above or create your own. Select an objective that is an action verb. Actors sometimes choose scenarios or adjectives instead of do-able actions.

Set the camera at eye level, and shoot three times. Actors choose three contrasting objectives to play.

Take 1. Wide shot

Choose one objective and play your objective to the mini-screen that is located on the right side of most cameras. As in the exercise before, play your objective with the intensity of a ten out of ten. Drive the stakes high. Play for life and death. Speak to the mini-viewing screen as if to a scene partner improvising your objective. Keep your awareness that you're playing for a wide shot and fill the entire screen with information, doing what you need to fulfill your objective.

Take 2. Medium shot

Choose a contrasting objective. The frame is smaller now, so focus your performance to fit the screen.

Take 3. Close-up

Choose yet a different contrasting objective, but this time play it silently without speech. Be aware of the screen size, so that you don't pop out of frame. Find stillness while fighting for your goal. Play in the eyes. Be like Medusa and kill with your eyes.

Note: don't worry if your objective isn't exactly clear to the audience, as long as it's clear to you. The filmmaker must provide context for your objectives. When you have a purpose, that aim drives the scene, whatever the context may be.

After going through these three takes, watch the tape and evaluate your performance.

Take 1

Is the actor filling the screen?
Are the stakes high which drive the objective?

Take 2

Has the performance changed to adapt to screen size?
Is the actor playing his objective at a ten?

Take 3

Is the actor playing in the eyes?
Is the silent performance effective?
Is the actor 'stated?'

Exercise 6. Strategies

This exercise emphasizes a character's strategy.

Work in pairs. Actor A is on screen, telephoning Actor B.

Set up a situation where A wants something from B. For example, A has just finished a late shift at work and it's raining. A wants B (her boyfriend or girlfriend) to get out of bed and to pick her up. B will not come to pick A up until she has persuasively used at least three different strategies. Strategies could include:

1. A tries to get B to feel sorry for her. 'It's wet, I'm cold and tired' etc.

2. A threatens B. 'I'm going to break up with you unless you come and pick me up.'

3. A bargains with B. 'I'll give you a little surprise if you come pick me up.'

Watch the performance. This is an exercise that practices playing different tactics and strategies to achieve an objective. Your character wants or needs something from the other character. When evaluating the performance ask:

* Were there three clear strategies to reach the objective?

* Were the strategies believable and persuasive?

* Was there contrast in the performance with each different strategy?

Exercise 7. 'Get out of the chair'

I'll only get out of the chair when I believe you.

Shoot this exercise with Actor B sitting directly next to the lens and Actor A in front of camera.

Actor A's objective is to get Actor B to stand up from the chair. Actor A can use whatever tactics necessary but Actor B will not get up out of the chair until he believes him. That means that he must see truth in Actor A's eyes.

Watch the tape and evaluate. The camera doesn't lie. Were you convinced by your own performance? This exercise can be repeated many times.

Exercise 8. Cold reading

Cold reading exercise A

Pick up a short magazine article or print advertisement and read it out loud. Now read the same article again but this time read it as though you need to sell the idea. Your loved one is ill and if you don't sell this idea to the camera, then your loved one will die.

Read it again, but this time you're seducing the camera with the written speech. You're wildly in lust with the camera and you need the camera to fall into lust with you too. You want the camera to go to bed with you.

Read the same article again but this time punish the camera.

Practice this exercises whenever you get a chance because the more you simply read out loud the more comfortable you will feel with it. I especially recommend this to actors who wish to audition in a language that is not their mother tongue. Even if you are fluent, cold reading in a foreign language often sounds robotic. This exercise will improve your ability to sight read more fluently.

> **Tip**
>
> Keep the script close rather than in your lap. If the script is in your lap, your eyes have too far to go, but not so close that the script blocks your face however. (See Figure V.2.)

Cold reading exercise B

If you're not working, meet with actor friends and work informally together. Reading a play that you've never read before out loud is an excellent way to practice cold reading, and familiarize yourself with world drama as well. You can switch characters around in each scene if you want practice playing different roles.

Tips for sight-reading at castings

* Remember that you don't have to completely cold read if you don't feel comfortable with it. If a caster thrusts a page into your hand, ask to take it into the hall for a few moments while they see someone else, and then come back in.

* Hold the script high (but not in front of your face). If the shot is in close up, we won't see the script in the shot anyway, but even if we do, so what? It's a cold read. If you hold the script low, your eyes have to go further down to find the words, and we'll just see your eyelids.

* Listen and don't read the other character's lines. We need to see your reaction. That will be the most interesting part of your performance

* To save your place on the page, as you listen, keep your thumb in the margin on the dialogue that is currently being read and keep it moving down the script as you progress.

Figure V.2. How not to hold the script

Dyslexia

Many actors are dyslexics and they tend to be very good at memorizing lines quickly to compensate. If you are dyslexic, let the casting director know in advance so we'll be sensitive about not throwing you a random text. If you are given a new script and asked to read it cold, ask if you can have a few moments with it.

Exercise 9. Telling a story

Work in pairs, off camera. Choose a theme and think of a particular moment in your life. Themes could include:

— something very embarrassing
— a time when you got caught
— something that happened to you when you were a child that changed your life

Tell your partner the story.

Listen carefully and empathetically to your partner's story, memorizing each detail.

Now work on camera. Tell your partner's story (not yours), in the first person, to the camera. Change a few details (of gender if needs be) to make the story work.

After going through this exercise, evaluate your performance. This exercise encapsulates the essence of acting. You're telling someone else's story, as if it were your own. This scene should reflect you and your personality. Were you able to convincingly and naturally tell your partner's story? Did we believe that it was your story? Was it an honest performance?

Part 6
Scene analysis

In this section, there are scenes from projects I have cast. You can use these scenes either for practice in front of the camera or to exercise your written scene analysis. Normally the casting director will provide the agent with a brief plot synopsis. Other times the project is so secretive that you know almost nothing and have to go make choices, based on the information on the written page, and instincts.

For each scene ask the following questions:

1. Who am I?
Start with the character's basic identity. I am ... It's OK if you don't know a great detail about the character. You can probably get everything you need from the scene.

2. Where am I?
It says this right at the top of the scene. Note whether it's interior (INT) or exterior (EXT). It will affect how you play the scene. Is it a public space like a restaurant or a private space like a bedroom? Are there other characters there watching you?

3. Who am I talking to?
Establish what your relationship with the other character is. You need or want something from them. Figure out what that is and relate it to your objective.

4. What do I want? The objective
This is the most important question because your answer will dictate how you play the scene. Surprisingly actors often neglect to answer this basic question. If you don't want something then you've got nothing to play. Choose an action verb that excites you.

5. What are the stakes?
What risk is your character taking? What does your character have to lose? This gives us the urgency or the tone in the scene. Choose the highest stakes that the context allows.

6. Where does the scene change?
The camera loves contrast and change. In any well-written scene, there is a transformative moment; something on which the scene hinges. Often it's marked by a moment of discovery, when the character learns or decides something. Choose where that is and mark it on your script. You don't have to plan *how* you'll change but know that there is a change. Here is an opportunity to play opposites. If the scene is about attraction, it is also about repulsion, for example.

7. What are the special technical or character considerations for playing this scene?

Ask yourself what props, if any, might help your performance. Think about the geography of the scene and where you will place off camera items to which the scene refers.

8. What page are we on in the script?

Normally a script is 100–120 pages. The page number tells us where we are in the story. This can be helpful when you consider the actor as storyteller. Although the character isn't aware, actors should know that they are telling a story. If we're on page 11, it's the first meeting of the romantic leads. Think about where they are going. If it's page 89, it's one of those the final scenes when the monster finally reveals itself to man. How desperate is the character at this point in the story?

9. What genre is this piece?

You should have this information in advance, but when you're not sure, ask. I was casting a black comedy once, and a number of actors who came in weren't aware that it was a comedy. When the actors were missing the jokes, then so did we. If it's a comedy, find the punch lines and punch them. If it's a historical drama, do some research on the period. If it's based on a comic book, read it and then don't worry about doing a long, thorough, Freudian analysis of your character. The bad guy in these films is just the bad guy. If you're a vampire, then your objective is to suck the other character's blood. Don't make it any more complicated than that.

Use the following evaluation form (below) when watching the playback for your scene. Learn to evaluate your work.

On Screen Acting Evaluation

	Poor	OK	Good	V. good	Excellent
Is the actor playing a clear objective?					
Is the actor listening?					
Is there a clear and varied inner monologue?					
Does the actor make a discovery or change?					
Does the actor play in the eyes?					

Where does the actor fall on a scale between over-acting and dead-face?

Deadface	Over-acting
This actor can take more risks	This actor can internalize the performance more

The Bourne Identity
Universal Pictures
Screenplay by *Tony Gilroy* and *W. Blake Herron*
Director *Doug Liman*

By the time I began working on this film, these main roles, played by Matt Damon and Franke Potente, had already been cast. The script was constantly changing and sometimes the director's assistant would call me during a casting session and read me the newly changed lines of the script over the phone (it was before the days of Blackberries). Like Bourne in the film itself, the production was flying by the seat of its pants. On the very last day of shooting, when I thought my job was done, the producer called and told me that I had to cast a new character because they realized that the end wasn't working and they needed to add a scene.

Scene I

25

58 Ext. Consulate/alleyway — day

MARIE *leaving her disastrous consulate encounter. She's broke — trapped — homeless —*

A LITTLE RED CAR. *A beat-to-shit Euro car. A shitty little red car angled in beside a dumpster with a big red Zurich parking ticket on the windshield —*

MARIE *[pulling the ticket]*

MARIE: *[Looking up —] [What are you looking at?]*

BOURNE *[standing across the car — on the passenger side —]*

BOURNE: I heard you inside.

MARIE: *[What?]*

BOURNE: The consulate. I heard you talking. *[beat]* I thought we could help each other out.

MARIE: How's that?

BOURNE: You need money. I need a ride out of here.

MARIE: *[firm to Bourne now —]* I'm not running a car service just now — thank you — goodbye . . . *[starting into the car —]*

> BOURNE: I'll give you ten thousand dollars to drive me to
>   Paris.
>
> MARIE: Great. You know what? I'll give you ten *billion* dollars to
>   get away from me before I start screaming.
>
> BOURNE   [*reaches into the bag — pulls out a stack of hundreds —
>   holding it —*]
>
> BOURNE: Ten thousand dollars. Drive me to Paris, it's
>   yours.
>
> MARIE: What is this? [*looking around —*] A joke? Some kind
>   of scam?
>
> BOURNE: No scam. Get me to Paris, the money's yours.
>
> MARIE [*— thinks quick — he's tossing the stack of hundreds at her
>   — she's almost dropping her satchel trying to catch it — but
>   there it is, in her hand —*]
>
> MARIE: Jesus . . .
>
> BOURNE: Look, I really need the ride.

Scene analysis for Marie

Who am I? I am Marie.

This side actually tells us a lot that we need to know about the character. 'MARIE leaving her disastrous consulate encounter. She's broke — trapped — homeless.' We don't know what the disastrous encounter was but can guess it probably had something to do with money and it's affected her well-being. We know that she's not having a good day. She drives a beaten-up car so she's probably down on her luck.

Where am I? I'm in a Zurich parking lot outside of the consulate.

EXT means that the scene is an exterior. It's in a public space where other people could be watching. That will effect how the scene is played.

Who am I talking to? I'm talking to a stranger.

Since the film is such a successful series now, most of us know who Bourne is. But if you were an actor getting the scene before the first film was made, you might not know. You could read the book *Bourne Identity*, but if you didn't have time, you still have the information you need to play the scene. (Actually the film was quite different from the book.) It seems like they noticed each other in the consulate, so Marie has seen him before, but he's still a stranger. Marie clearly doesn't trust him at first. Why should she?

What do I want? I want to get into my car and drive away.

Keep the objective very simple. She's at her car in a parking lot. When Bourne appears the objective changes. Her objective could be to protect herself from the stranger ('Get away from me.'), or more actively, to confront him ('How dare you?'), to ridicule him ('Yeah right, you have $10,000!').

Where does the scene change? The scene changes when Bourne offers me the money. Ten thousand dollars means a lot to someone who is broke. Don't throw this bit away. This is the transitional part of the scene, when she says 'Jesus'. Take a moment to see the money, feel it in your hands and take in its importance.

What are the stakes? Personal safety verses financial reward. She needs the money desperately, but can she trust this handsome stranger?

Technical considerations

Props could really be helpful in this scene. If you don't feel comfortable miming, you can use some basic props that are easy to bring with you. If her objective is to get into her car, what does she need? She needs her keys, of course. The actor could bring in her own handbag, using it as a prop to dig around in to find the keys. The other crucial prop is the bag of money. Consider if you want to mime this or respond to something real.

What page are we on? We're on page 25. Since there are usually 110 pages or so in a script, that means we are at the beginning of the film. These characters are meeting for the first time and starting a relationship. Could there be a flicker of chemistry?

Character considerations

Marie is the female romantic lead. The audience is meeting her for the first time. Although it's a serious scene and the character is in a bad mood, remember that she can have a sense of humor too. The audience wants to like this character and be on her side.

Scene analysis for Bourne

We've all seen Matt Damon do this but try not to let him influence your choices. For the sake of this exercise, let's say that the studio is producing a re-make and wants to find an unknown to play Bourne.

Who am I? I am Bourne, a secret government agent, with a bad case of amnesia.

He knows almost nothing about himself, except that the next clue to figuring out his identity is in Paris. He's just run from the consulate after a close brush with death.

Where am I? I am in a Zurich parking lot, outside the embassy.

Where has he been? He's just run from the consulate where Marines were shooting at him. They are still in the area, so Bourne is probably nervous about standing in clear view for too long.

Who am I talking to? Marie is the helpless girl who I pinpointed in the consulate.

She has something that Bourne needs — a car. His relationship to her at this point in the film is as one of mutual need. He's identified quickly that she's broke. He's thinking fast and he's thinking on his feet.

What do I want? I want a ride to Paris.

It's quite simple and Bourne says it, 'I really need the ride'. The scene could be boiled down to the one and final line.

Where does the scene change? When I show her the money. This is the deal breaker.

What's at stake? Life and death. 'If I stay here, I'll be shot.'

Technical considerations

Props, like a bag of money, could be helpful but not essential for playing this scene. There is no need for a lot of extraneous movement or blocking.

What page are we on? 25. It's very early in Bourne's journey. He's still disoriented.

Character considerations

The challenge for this character is to get what he wants, without scaring Marie. We have to believe that she'd give him the ride. He can't play the objective so strongly that no woman traveling alone would let him into her car. How can you display the right amount of vulnerability, yet urgency? Remember too that his plan is spontaneous. Bourne doesn't have time to premeditate. He is constantly thinking on his feet. Bring this into the performance.

What is the genre? It's an action/adventure movie. Does this matter to the actor? Yes, this scene has to move just like the movie has to move. No director wants to sit around while you make tons of beats and pauses.

Anne Frank: The Whole Story
ABC Mini Series
Screenplay by *Kirk Ellis*
Director *Robert Dornhelm*

This project exemplified a globalized approach to casting and international cooperation. It was produced by Americans, shot in Prague, with an Austrian-American director, Robert Dornhelm, and German-American producer, Hans Proppe. We had an international team of casting directors headed by Meg Liberman in LA, Suzanne Smith in London, Job Goschalk and Saida van der Reijd in Amsterdam, the late Risa Kes in Munich and my associate Minna Pyyhkala and myself in Prague. It was wonderful for us to be recognized for our work with an Emmy nomination. We cast quite a few supporting roles from Prague, but thankfully the Dutch characters in this scene were cast in Amsterdam.

Scene II
Anne Frank (Night Two)   225

227 Int. 263 Prinsengracht — Kugler's office — continuous

The wallet drops onto Kugler's desk. Kugler looks up in surprise at Van Maaren.

MIEP: [*racing in*] I'm sorry, Mr. Kugler. This man just—

KUGLER: It's alright, Miep. I'll deal with Mr. Van Maaren.

Miep glares at Van Maaren as she withdraws. She closes the door behind her. Kugler calmly scoops the wallet off his desk and stuffs it in his jacket pocket.

KUGLER: [*cont'd*] I was wondering where that had gotten to. Thank you.

VAN MAAREN: So it's your wallet, then is it?

KUGLER: I've just told you.

VAN MAAREN: You were in the warehouse last night.

KUGLER: That's right.

VAN MAAREN: Why?

KUGLER: Look here — I don't have to explain myself to you.

VAN MAAREN: Did a certain Mr. Frank work in this office at one time? A Jew?

KUGLER: What's that got to do with anything?

VAN MAAREN: What happened to him?

KUGLER: He — disappeared.

VAN MAAREN: Disappeared.

KUGLER: That's right. Now if you'll excuse me—

Kugler crosses to the door and holds it open.

KUGLER: [*cont'd*] If it's a reward you're looking for, I'm sorry to disappoint you.

VAN MAAREN: Oh, I've got my reward, all right.

Van Maaren smiles. Kugler can see the man knows something, but meets his gaze evenly.

Scene analysis for Kugler

Who am I? I am Mr. Kugler.

Most of us already know the story of Anne Frank, the Jewish girl who hid in an attic during the Second World War. Even if we haven't read the script and have no further information about the character, we can gather that Kugler is one of the Dutch characters who is hiding the Frank family. He works at a desk in an office, so we infer that he has a white collar, management position.

Where am I? In my office on Prinsengacht Street. INT means that it's inside.

Who am I talking to? I'm talking to my worker, Van Maaren, who has found Otto Frank's wallet.

What do I want? There are a number of active objectives that an actor can choose to play in this scene.

Overall the character's objective is to protect the Frank family from the Nazis. It's unclear if this worker, Van Maaren, is a direct threat to the family or not. He definitely is starting to put the pieces of a puzzle together that could betray Kugler as well as the Franks. Among the active objectives an actor could choose to play are:

❋ to persuade Van Maaren that all is normal

❋ to put Van Maaren in his place

❋ to keep the upper hand in his relationship as Van Maaren's employer

❋ to dismiss Van Maaren

Metaphorically he is playing a game of poker with Van Maaren, and can't let the other players see his cards.*

What are the stakes? Life and death.

If Van Maaren reports that Kugler is hiding Jews, then Kugler can go to the death camps as well.

---

* Actors often choose 'to protect' or 'to conceal' — both are true but you need a positive action to play, as well.

Where does the scene change? This scene is subtle compared to the other scenes I present in this section.

My choice would be when Van Maaren says, 'Did a certain Mr. Frank work here, a Jew?' For Kugler, this is when he knows for sure that Van Maaren knows something incriminating. The external change could be imperceptible though because Kugler doesn't want Van Maaren to see him twitch.

Technical considerations

Kugler is sitting at a desk. You might not be able to get a table in front of you, but a few props, like some work paper (your script, for example) and a pencil could be useful. Maybe Kugler pretends to go back to his work at one point when he dismisses Van Maaren.

Character considerations

This character is lying when he pretends that it's his wallet. We're more than half way through the script and Kugler is still alive, so he's already had to lie a number of times to protect the family. In this scene you're an actor, playing an actor. He is probably a good actor just like you are. You don't have to project his discomfort. The audience will feel uncomfortable already.

Since there is a lot of subtext, actors sometimes try to show the subtext too much. Trust that the audience will get it. Let the text carry the story, and keep it simple.

Scene analysis for Van Maaren

Who am I? I am a blue collar Dutchman who works at Kugler's Warehouse during World War II.

Who am I talking to? I'm talking to my boss, Mr. Kugler

What do I want? I want to return a wallet to him that I've found. As we learned in Kugler's analysis, there are many choices the actor could make in a scene such as this. These choices are based on motives.

* to blackmail Kugler (I know he's guilty and I want to use this information to blackmail my boss)

* to incriminate Kugler (I know he's guilty and I will report him)

* to warn Kugler (I'm scared for myself and my family. I don't want to be part of this plot to hide Jews)

Any of these choices could work. Try two different approaches and see how they change the scene. It's a good idea to come in with at least two ideas in case they ask you to try it a different way.

What are the stakes? The stakes depend on what choice the actor makes.

If he's afraid that he will go down with Kugler for hiding Jews, then the stakes are life or death for him too. If he sees this as an opportunity to blackmail his boss, then the stakes are money and power. What can he gain?

Where does the scene change? For Van Maaren, the scene could change quite early. He knows it's Otto Frank's wallet that he has found. When Kugler pretends that it's his wallet, Van Maaren knows that he is lying.

Character considerations

Van Maaren is not the culprit in the script who turns the Franks in. He is not necessarily the bad guy. Actors are tempted to play Van Maaren as an evil, mustache-twisting villain. This is a realistic, historical drama. It's about real people in real situations.

Questions for both characters

What page of the script are we on? It says Night Two at the top of the page, and we're on page 225. That means we are at the beginning of the second night of a two night mini-series. We're just over half way through. We know that the Franks are eventually turned in. Tension is building in the story as their hide-away is starting to crack open.

What is the genre? It's a TV mini-series, and it's a factual historical drama. Ideally you should read Melissa Muller's book, on which the film is based, and *Anne Frank: The Diary of a Young Girl*. In a TV script, there is generally more text than in a film, where the story is told with images. TV producers need to keep the audience engaged even when their attention is not on the screen so the dialogue is important. It's a historical drama and these characters are based on real people, that actors can research. If there is limited time before the casting, the actor should at the very least find a synopsis of the story, and learn a little bit about the period and place.

Alien Vs. Predator
20th Century Fox
Written by *Dan O'Bannon* and *Ronald Shusett*
Directed by *Paul Anderson*

When I first came onto the project I asked director, Paul Anderson, if we were casting any stars, and he said, 'There are two stars already in this movie. Alien and Predator'. Consequently, it provided excellent opportunities for actors who weren't famous to get a break. Scenes that take place right at the moment of death, like the one below, are challenging to play. Since I usually cast only supporting cast, I end up casting a lot of dying scenes since the characters who live are cast out of Los Angeles and the ones who die are cast regionally. The actors who read for this scene had certainly not read the script since it was top secret. Once I had started auditioning casting director Suzanne Smith called from London and asked me to black out the part of the scene that describes the face hugger grabbing Jamison's face because production didn't want to give away the surprise of the scene. (I agreed but the fate of these characters seemed pretty obvious to me.) If you have seen the finished version of this film, you will notice that the scene is different, with the names of the characters changed and most of the dialogue trimmed out.

Scene III

Int. pyramid — Sacrificial Chamber   78.

ALBRECHT, JAMISON *and five other* SCIENTISTS *struggle with the stone blocking the entrance. Their attempts are in vain*

JAMISON: Slab's gotta weigh two tons. We'll never move it.
Albrecht looks around. Right now he's feeling very scared and extremely claustrophobic.
ALBRECHT: I don't like this. I don't like this at all.
We are screwed. We are so incredibly screwed.
We are never going to get out of here.
JAMISON: Well, you can't click your heels to get back home Albrecht, so why don't you start using that big brain of yours to get us out of here.
Albrecht's eyes have found something.
ALBRECHT: That egg wasn't there a minute ago.
On one of the sacrificial slabs, an ALIEN EGG *suddenly appears. It sits snugly in the bow shaped indentation, which Lex had observed earlier. The stone slabs themselves are silently splitting apart, allowing the Alien Eggs to rise up into the indentation from within. More and more, the whole Pyramid is starting to resemble some kind of giant machine.*
JAMISON: There . . . another.
ALBRECHT: One more.
Now all seven sacrificial slabs have an Egg on them. There is a long silence. Then the first Egg begins to open. [ON JAMISON]
Unseen by the others, a COLT.45 *slides out of her Weyland Industries jacket sleeve and into her hand.*
ALBRECHT: [*staring at the Eggs*] What are those things?
One by one the other Eggs begin to open
JAMISON: What did you say this room was called Professor?

ALBRECHT: [*scared*] The Sacrificial Chamber.

Jamison brings up her HANDGUN *and* FIRES. *And in a split second, the Face Hugger completes its flight. Slamming into Jamison's face, smothering her mouth . . . muffling her screams.*

Scene analysis for Jamison

Who am I? I am Jamison, a woman who fights aliens.

If all you have from the script is this scene, you can gather that she is the leader of this team who is investigating, because she commands Albrecht. She carries a gun and knows how to use it. She could be military or former military. She's is a courageous woman, who is facing her fears and acting pragmatically to resolve the situation. A reference for this character could be Sigourney Weaver in the first *Alien* movie.

Where am I? I'm in the sacrificial chamber in a pyramid.

We know this because Albrecht says so. It's not a great place to be.

Who are you talking to? I am talking to Albrecht.

What do you know about Albrecht from this scene? She thinks he's smarter because she says that he's the one with the 'big brains,' who needs to 'think' to get her 'out of here'. Perhaps he's a professor or scientist. What does she need from him? She needs his help, his brains, for survival.

What do I want? I want to survive.

In a scene like this it's pretty easy to figure out what you want. She needs to escape the sacrificial chamber. It's helpful to ask a follow-up question as well. *What does the character do to get what she wants?* The character has three strategies. The first step is physical; she's pushing a stone to remove a physical obstacle. Step two is that she needs something from the other character. She needs Albrecht to calm down. If he can think clearly, then she has a chance. Step three comes after the scene changes. The eggs are appearing. So now she uses her gun and shoots at them.

Where does the scene change? The scene changes when there is a clear and present threat — the eggs appear. You might have had a chance up until that point.

What are the stakes? The stakes are life or death.

She's in a sacrificial chamber with a bunch of aliens. It doesn't get any worse than that. In the casting, we have to believe that you believe that these are the last moments of your life.

Technical considerations

You're playing the moment before death. The challenge is that you have nothing to play off of in the room. There is no alien to scare the life out of you, and there won't be on set. Some geek at a computer will create that later. So you have to use your imagination to fill in all the details yourself. Actors like Angelina Jolie or Bruce Willis make action look easy but action scenes often throw actors in castings. There is very little dialogue so you have to break the scene down and play the actions and the moments between the words.

You might want to give yourself something physical, like a chair, to push against in the beginning. When the eggs appear, figure out exactly where they are. Be specific and really see each egg. You have to see them in a specific place. If you put them off to the side, your head goes profile. If you put them on the ground, your eyes go down and we see your eyelids. We need to see the fear in your eyes because that's what the scene is about. Place the eggs right around the camera lens. When you're dying we need to see the fear in your eyes at the moment before death so keep playing to camera.

This character operates a gun. If you want to play action, research how to hold and shoot a gun. These details make it convincing. Be sure that your physical actions are clear and precise. Focus on the specific actions and play them with an economy of movement.

Scene analysis for Albrecht

Who am I? I am Albrecht.

He's got the 'brain' so he's probably some kind of scientist or professor.

Where am I? I'm in the sacrificial chamber in a pyramid that we're exploring.

Who am I talking to? I'm talking to Jamison, the leader of the mission. I want her to protect me.

What do I want? I want to survive the sacrificial chamber.

Like Jamison, Albrecht is fighting to unblock the stone. For Albrecht the analysis of the scene is much the same. His reaction to the eggs might be quite different to Jamison's. She has a gun and he doesn't. If he's a scientist, maybe he's initially interested in the eggs. Here is an opportunity to play an opposite. He can go from playing 'to fight for an escape', to 'discovering' these fascinating eggs. This is the kind of interesting choice that can make a performance stand out. Instead of just playing scared the whole time, find an unexpected moment.

What are the stakes? Life and death.

Where does the scene change? 'The Sacrificial Chamber.'

The line, 'the sacrificial chamber', could be the turning point for Albrecht (rather than the appearance of the eggs). Something is dawning on him. Another choice is that the irony of the situation actually occurs to him. If the audience can have a sense of irony then so can the characters. He realizes that they will be sacrificed in the sacrificial chamber.

Technical considerations

See the notes for Jamison above. Although you don't operate a gun in the scene, you do have to really see the eggs and make them real.

Actors often hyperventilate during these scared scenes. It might be what people do when they are frightened, but it doesn't work on camera. You don't have to force the fear out.

Analysis for both characters

What page are we on in the script? Page 59

We're about half way through the story. The tension is starting to build. The characters probably know that there are creatures but they haven't seen them yet.

What genre is this piece? This is a science fiction/horror film.

The acting in these films is every bit as real as it would be in a drama. The challenge for the actor is that you have only your own resources to draw from. On set, the alien was represented by the assistant director pulling a broom around to indicate where the alien was.

Euro Trip
DreamWorks
Written by *Alec Berg, David Mandel* and *Jeff Schaffer*

Euro Trip was a scream to work on. The three writers were a solid team who had co-written Seinfeld episodes among other things and, although (for reasons having to do with the director's guild) only Jeff Schaffer claimed director credit, they actually directed as a team. Before working with them, I was afraid that they wouldn't be able to agree on anything but that wasn't the case. They loved looking at casting tapes and laughed out loud when their jokes worked. They met many actors in Prague and all over Europe.

Scene V

92

80 Int. Vip room — night

JENNY *and* CHRISTOPH *clinking champagne flutes in a romantic corner staring into each other's eyes*

JENNY: This place is amazing. I can't believe you own all these nightclubs.

CHRISTOPH: My older brother runs the family shipping and banking interests, and I guess you could say I'm the black sheep of the family.

JENNY: No, you're not. Besides if you were off doing all that banking and shipping, we wouldn't be here right now. Well, you wouldn't.

He moves in close, takes her hand.

CHRISTOPH: Jennifer. I realize that we have only just met, but I feel such a connection with you.

JENNY: You do? I do, too. Totally.

CHRISTOPH: My family has a yacht on the Aegean. Come with me Jennifer. We will sail away together.

JENNY: Oh my God . . .

Jenny swoons. Is this really happening?

CHRISTOPH: We will swim with dolphins and sip champagne by moonlight.

JENNY: Oh my God . . .

CHRISTOPH: We will spend the days sunbathing and drinking wine. My wife makes the best sangria.

JENNY: Oh, my God — wait what?

CHRISTOPH: Sangria. You take a good Spanish Rioja and put in slices of orange, and apple—

JENNY: No, no. You're married? But the moonlight, and the dolphins . . . I thought you wanted to . . .

CHRISTOPH: Have sex? Yes, of course we will. You, me and my wife. And maybe my wife's sister.

JENNY: Ugh. That's gross.

CHRISTOPH: No, it is European.

JENNY: So you just run around Europe sleeping with any woman you meet?

CHRISTOPH: Please Jennifer, it is not like that, I also sleep with men. Last month my wife's brother visited the yacht —

JENNY: Ugh! I'm going to be sick.

She throws a drink on him, grabs another drink from a passing waitress and throws that on him too. She storms out, leaving a wet CHRISTOPH *and the waiter stunned*

Christoph sighs, then turns to the waiter, smooth as ever, speaks in a foreign language.

CHRISTOPH: [*subtitled*] You see that Eurasian girl by the bar? Send her a sangria . . .

Scene analysis for Jenny

Who am I? I am a young American girl traveling in Europe.

Where am I? I'm in the VIP room in a European club.

It is a public but interior scene. She's sitting in a cozy corner, and from the text 'this place is amazing', she is pretty impressed with the club.

Who am I talking to? I'm talking to Christoph, a wealthy, yacht owning, European man.

Do we think he's telling the truth? It doesn't matter. Jenny thinks so. His promises to take her to his yacht are fulfilling all of her girlhood fantasies about a dashing European man, on a white horse who will sweep her off her feet.

What do I want? I want him.

She wants him as the answer to her prayers. He's the man who will love her, show her a perfect life, and yes, he will marry her! She can't wait to invite her friends to the yacht. She's about ready to call her mother and tell her to choose a wedding dress.

Where does the scene change? The wife.

Everything was going pretty well until he mentions a wife and then it plummets steeply downhill. This guy goes from married, to incestuous, to homosexual. If she lets him continue, he might suggest having sex with a pony. The mention of the wife is the important moment for Jenny to play opposites going from gooey-eyed to disgusted. This scene is perfectly written in that sense. Attraction–Repulsion. Her objective changes from, 'I want to marry him' to 'I want to confront him' or 'punish him'.

What are the stakes? Comedy is about pain.

Although everyone has heard the phrase 'We're not laughing at you, we're laughing *with* you', this is not true in comedy. We're usually laughing *at* someone's pain and in this case it is Jenny's pain. The higher the stakes, the farther she'll fall and the funnier the scene is. This is why I would advise actors to make the objective marriage, rather than just a fun night. Jenny wants him to sweep her off her feet. She believes that he is the romantic prince that he originally appears to be. What's at stake is a loss of that fantasy, and the hurtful disappointment that Christoph is a pervert.

Technical considerations

Although the scene indicates that it be shot with the actors sitting next to each other on a couch, be prepared to read the scene facing the camera, with the reader to the right or left of the lens. Don't count on the reader holding your hand or giving you anything to spring from, other than the lines themselves. For heaven sakes *take* your exit. Don't miss a great exiting line.

Find the punch lines. In a script like this, you've got to identify the jokes and tell them. In comedic terms, Jenny is playing the straight man. He sets up the jokes and she makes them work by how she reacts to them. Actor and comedian Steve Carell says, 'I love comedies where the characters don't know they're in a comedy'. So play it like realism and the pain will be real and the comedy will work.

Scene analysis for Christoph

Who am I? I am a European nightclub owner.

Since we don't know what country he's from, it probably doesn't matter so just use your own accent, if you are European. If you aren't, then ask if the accent is important.

Where am I? In the VIP room of my club.

INT, with other people present.

Who am I talking to? Jenny is an attractive American girl.

What do I want? I want to convince her to participate in my orgy.

Where does the scene change? 'Oh that's gross.'

While for Jenny the scene changes when he mentions that he's married, for Christoph the scene changes when he starts to realize he won't get what he wants. Before Jenny says 'that's gross' he has a chance. His objective could change from 'to convince' to 'prove to her that this is normal European behavior'.

What are the stakes? Sex.

If comedy is about pain then what is Christoph's pain? What is at stake for him is sex. Is sex important? Yes, for this character it certainly is. The comedy comes from his disappointment, but also from his cluelessness about American tastes. In his world, it is normal to have these kind of orgies. If you play the scene sincerely, that you really believe that this is normal European behavior, the comedy works.

Technical considerations

Don't count on being able to use touch or to have an actress next to you on a couch. It's all you and your charm in front of camera.

When Jenny throws the drink in your face and storms off, you have an opportunity to be on camera for a few seconds on your own. Maybe at this moment we see the real Christoph - the Christoph who isn't putting a show on for the ladies. Take the time to play the transition from disappointment to hope again once you identify another target (the Eurasian girl).

Consideration for both characters

Pace is always a consideration in comedy; ere on the side of quick pacing. Comedy is almost never slow.

What is the genre? This is a well-written comedy. Find the jokes and tell them.

What page are we on? 92.

It's late in the script so Jenny has probably had quite a few European adventures already. She's getting fed up with Europeans and ready to go home. It matters less for Christoph since he is a cameo character.

Conclusion

When you get the role

Congratulations! You booked the role. Now your goal is to do great work on set so that you work again. Film is arguably the most collaborative of art forms. Actors who cooperate and make an effort to understand other crew members' jobs will be appreciated. You may give a stellar performance but if you make a problem for the crew, the casting director will inevitably hear about it. The sad fact is that I more often get a call from production when there is a problem. If you were brilliant, I may not hear a word. One actor I cast turned up on set drunk. He now frequently drops off his headshots in my office but seems puzzled that I don't invite him for auditions. We also get irate calls if an actor has lied about her horse riding ability. If you lie about your skills, no one will love you on set, and no will love me for hiring you. I am unlikely to stake my reputation on you again.

Keep in mind that the techniques in this book are suggested with auditioning in mind. While I encourage actors to play with the text and make different choices during the casting process, remember that on set, performance must be fresh but consistent so that shots will match. You have to be one hundred percent aware of your continuity, remembering to put the phone down with the same hand each time, for example. Continuity is part of professional acting technique and the script supervisor will thank you for it. Collaborating also means helping other actors by being available off camera to provide an eye line.

Come prepared and ask questions when you don't understand. While I encourage actors to hold the script in hand during an audition, this is obviously not advisable on set. Know the lines cold. Memorize the facts and the intentions of the scene. A thorough approach to character development and script analysis is required. Read the entire script no matter how small or large your role is.

Production should send the screenplay but if they don't, ask your agent to request it as soon as the deal is made. The second assistant director is the first crew member you will have contact with, and she is your buddy.

Some actors return from set with a perplexed reaction to the shooting process, complaining that they got no feedback on their performance. If the director gives no notes, that probably means that your performance was fine. The director might have been thinking more about camera placement, or finishing her shoot day on time, than about the specifics of your performance. They hired you because they liked your performance during the audition; they may not want to provide acting notes on set.

If any of the advice in *Secrets from the Casting Couch* has helped you, please drop me a line because I'd love to know about it. Send your casting stories to my blog at www.nancybishopcasting.blogspot.com

Bibliography

Biskind, Peter. *Easy Riders, Raging Bulls; How the Sex 'n' Drugs 'n' Rock 'n' Roll Generation Saved Hollywood.* Bloomsbury, London, 1998.

Caine, Michael. *Acting in Film: An Actor's Take on Movie Making.* Applause Books, New York, 1997.

Chekhov, Michael. *To the Actor on the Technique of Acting.* Harper and Row, New York, 1953.

Gillespie, Bonnie. *Self-Management for Actors: Getting Down to (Show) Business.* Cricket Feet Publishing. Los Angeles, 2009

Hirshenson, Janet and Jenkins, Jane with Kranz, Rachel. *A Star is Found: Our Adventures Casting some of Hollywood's Biggest Movies.* A Harvest Book, Harcourt, Inc., San Diego 2006.

Hyde, Lewis. *The Gift: Creativity and the Artist in the Modern World.* Vintage Books USA, Random House, 2007.

Levitin, Daniel. *This is Your Brain on Music: The Science of a Human Obsession.* Penguin Group, 2006.

Mamet, David. *True and False: Heresy and Common Sense for the Actor.* Vintage Books, USA, Random House, New York, 1999.

Merlin, Joanna. *Auditioning: An Actor-Friendly Guide.* Vintage Books USA, Random House, New York, 2001.

Murch, Walter. *In the Blink of an Eye.* Silman-James Press, Los Angeles, 2001.

Stanislavski, Konstantin. Translated by Elizabeth Reynolds Hapgood. *Creating a Role.* Routledge, London, 1948.

Stanislavski, Konstantin. Translated by Elizabeth Reynolds Hapgood. *An Actor Prepares.* Routledge, London, 1948.

Shurtleff, Michael. *Audition: Everything an Actor Needs to Know to Get the Part.* Walker and Company, New York, 1978.

Tucker, Patrick. *Secrets of Screen Acting.* Theatre Arts Books, Routledge, 2003.

Weston, Judith. *Directing Actors: Creating Memorable Performances for Film and Television.* Michael Wiese Productions, 1996.

Index